METAPHYSIC OF EXPERIENCE
IN
ADVAITA VEDĀNTA

METAPHYSIC OF EXPERIENCE IN ADVAITA VEDĀNTA

A Phenomenological Approach

DEBABRATA SINHA

MOTILAL BANARSIDASS PUBLISHERS
PRIVATE LIMITED • DELHI

First Edition: Delhi, 1983
Reprint: Delhi, 1995

ISBN: 81-208-0942-4

Also available at:

MOTILAL BANARSIDASS

41 U.A. Bungalow Road, Jawahar Nagar, Delhi 110 007
120 Royapettah High Road, Mylapore, Madras 600 004
16 St. Mark's Road, Bangalore 560 001
Ashok Rajpath, Patna 800 004
Chowk, Varanasi 221 001

PRINTED IN INDIA
BY JAINENDRA PRAKASH JAIN AT SHRI JAINENDRA PRESS,
A-45 NARAINA, PHASE I, NEW DELHI 110 028
AND PUBLISHED BY NARENDRA PRAKASH JAIN FOR
MOTILAL BANARSIDASS PUBLISHERS PRIVATE LIMITED,
BUNGALOW ROAD, DELHI 110 007

CONTENTS

PREFACE

To the Revised Edition

This book is a modified edition of my previous work published under the title, *The Idealist Standpoint : A Study in the Vedāntic Metaphysic of Experience*. Although sharing with the original edition a very substantial identity of content, the present version nevertheless bears considerable omissions and reworkings of certain sections (including Introduction). If an apology for this renewed enterprise is at all to be cited, it is the need felt by the author in a certain measure for totally focusing on the theme itself, that is, the *Cit*-centric critique of experience in terms of Advaita Vedānta, without letting the otherwise pertinent but peripheral discussions of comparative (Western) perspectives interfere in the basic concern and thrust of the work. With that end in view, and possibly with a certain awareness of the 'anthropological' accent—that is, on human subjectivity rather than epistemological-transcendental subjectivity as such—in the interpretive understanding of the central philosophy of Advaitism, I have sought to restructure the original treatment of the subject-matter to an extent that would restore the full focus of this investigation—the major area of materials already embodied in the study having been left completely unaffected.

Further, the objective of making the work available for meeting the demand of an increasing number of interested and involved students and researchers—here at Brock, and elsewhere in North America and in India—provided an additional incentive to my endeavour to bring out the work afresh. In doing so, I have certainly drawn encouragement from many appreciative reviews and responses on the book (in its earlier form) coming forth over the years since its publication in 1965.

Finally, I owe it to Motilal Banarsidass—Messrs. N. P. and J. P. Jain in particular—to take over the publication of the present volume most readily.

St. Catharines
April, 1982

DEBABRATA SINHA

PREFACE

To the original Edition

The search after 'a new name for some old ways of thinking' —as William James preferred to characterize 'Pragmatism'—may be said to represent, in one sense, the philosophic endeavour of the modern mind. New names need not be a question of mere nomenclature, but also be looked upon as a genuine way of thinking itself. Through such thinking alone can the older systems of thought undergo the process of being re-integrated to the living currents of present thinking. And this process should be taken as one organic to true philosophizing rather than as external to it. There may, after all, be no little truth in the Bradleyan epigram that "metaphysics is the finding of bad reasons for what is believed upon instinct". But the said 'instinct', i.e., the basic insight (or insights), constituting the foundation of a philosophical system, need not be taken as one unamenable to critical reasoning. Rather, philosophic reflection proper should be directed towards grasping such fundamentals without resting upon the externals of metaphysical arguments as such.

This attitude being taken into consideration, the present enquiry would proceed towards re-understanding one of the classical systems of Indian thought, viz., Advaita Vedānta. The latter has not been sought to be understood in this study as a finished specimen of antiquarian thought; there has rather been an attempt to arrive at the central standpoint which should offer a fuller understanding of Advaitic idealism. An exaggerated concern for the external argumentative superstructure of an old metaphysical system is apt to divert our attention from the standpoint that might have originally motivated the philosophic outlook of the system concerned. The scope for misunderstanding and misinterpretation in this regard would perhaps nowhere be greater than in the classical systems of India—developed as they have through centuries, from the earlier *Sūtrabhāṣya* stage to the later dialectical phase. But it can hardly be denied that the life-essence of a philosophical system does not lie in the sets of hypotheses put forward in abstraction.

I have been well aware that to attempt to re-interpret a classical system—particularly one so proved and developed as Śaṅkara's Vedānta—may well mean a rather embarassing task. So I have attempted here a free interpretation of what may be considered to be the principal tenet of Advaita, rather than a bare textual interpretation or a historical study. [In this—as well as in certain basic respects in the line of interpretation followed—I have been emboldened by at least one outstanding example, viz., that of the late Professor K. C. Bhattacharyya, who, as stated in the Introduction to his *Studies in Vedantism*, offers "problematic constructions on Vedantic lines intended to bring out the relations of the system to modern philosophical systems".] My central aim has indeed been directed to the fundamental standpoint in the light of which the edifice of Advaitic idealism may be sought to be understood and thus intelligibly reorganized. All that we may claim in the present study is not historic authenticity but a possible alternative way of understanding the central thesis of Advaita Vedānta in a new light.

What has engaged my interest throughout the work is the principle of Being as identified with Consciousness, to be found in the common Vedāntic doctrine of *Sat-Cit*. The doctrine of Being (*Sat*) has usually been approached in terms of formal arguments; but thereby the unique import of *Cit*, the principle of consciousness, has more often than not been missed. A mere abstract formulation of the principle of *Cit* in formal-metaphysical terms is apt to forgo its concrete bearing upon, and relation to, experience—what originally motivated Advaita as a *Cit*-centric philosophy, but is very often ignored in the common enunciation of *Cit* which joins it more or less in an abstract way to the principle of Being. On my reading, a far more illuminating way of approaching *Cit* in the light of interpretation of experience seems to lie in the notion of subjectivity. The latter alone could assure for Advaita a unique standpoint which may give way to a subjectively-oriented 'metaphysic of experience', to be retraced within the framework of the Advaita system itself.

Our enquiry begins by proposing a fresh approach in the matter of adequately understanding what may be (philosophically, not historically) the standpoint motivating the philosophical character of the system at hand—its general idealistic standpoint and outlook (Introduction). The four chapters of Part I have been employed in the establishment—on independent grounds—and elucidation of *Cit* as the principle of subjectivity *par excellence* (Ch. I). (In view of the possible opposition from the realistic-positivistic camp at large, the establishment of the standpoint concerned has taken a major share in our study.) Thus is prepared the ground for the next—and the central—part of the enquiry (Chs. V and VI), which attempts to work out the fuller implications of the principle of *Cit*—a principle that would lead ultimately to a more or less full-fledged criticism of experience.

However, an examination of the bare standpoint of subjectivity as such may further raise doubts as to whether the former could yield an *ontological* standpoint proper (the latter being the approach that has commonly been accepted as central to Advaita philosophy). Accordingly, the last part (2 chapters in Part III) takes up this question, and brings out the *alogical* transition to the standpoint of Being from that of 'transcendental subjectivity' in the form of *Cit*.

In my line of interpretation, which obviously is not committed to any agreement with the orthodox or the standard one, I have rather made free use of the Phenomenology of Edmund Husserl, which itself represents rather a heterodoxy in European thought. With its typical subjectively-oriented outlook, Phenomenology seems, of all the Western systems, to promise the closest approach to Advaitic idealism (in its *Cit*-aspect)—necessary concessions being, of course, made for the otherwise widely different contexts. And the methodology that Phenomenology offers may throw no little light towards a possible system of analysis of experience, attuned to the standpoint of subjectivity.

I might have as well stopped with Part II, where an outline of the Advaita metaphysic of experience has been attempted. But a demand for greater justice to the metaphysical standpoint as it actually occurs in Vedānta has eventually led to the concluding part—although it need not, strictly speaking, have come within the scope of our enquiry. The methodological approach adopted by us necessitates a so-called 'transition' to the metaphysical standpoint, although in Vedānta such a passage from one standpoint to the other would not evidently be entailed. I am keenly aware that our line of interpretation, deriving a possible metaphysic of experience, and therefrom an ontological scheme, might well be developed further—not merely in the Vedāntic context, but possibly in respect of some other classical systems too.

In spite of the relative freedom in the treatment of the original texts concerned, I have proceeded, as far as possible, with reference to the relevant Sanskrit literature of Advaita Vedānta—and of other schools on occasions. In freely drawing from the original texts, I have, however, been chiefly concerned with the philosophical interpretation of the relevant points rather than the exact reproduction of the arguments as such. Our sources on Vedānta have chiefly been drawn from the commentaries of Śaṅkarācārya and the works of the *Vivaraṇa* school in particular, including such later works as *Citsukhī* etc.

As regards Phenomenology, I have had to depend for the sources largely on the English translation of the first volume of Husserl's *Ideas* (that being the only available English version of the great bulk of Husserl's works, except the *Encyclopaedia Britannica* article, at the time of my preparing the work). The very nature of my work being an interpretation from within rather than an external comparison of the two schools, may explain my free use of the phenomenological terminology in the Vedāntic context (especially in Chapters V and VI). However, considering the necessity for a closer account of the salient features of Husserl's Phenomenology in the context of my investigations, I have preferred to append a brief Note on Phenomenology at the end. Some reference to Existentialism—a more or less allied movement and one no less heterodox than Phenomenology—is also called for, at least in the last chapter, by the very nature of our approach. But the compass of the present enquiry would hardly permit further treatment of Existentialism as such.

The present work is a revised and slightly abridged version of my thesis, originally submitted and accepted for the D. Phil.

degree in Philosophy of the Calcutta University. On this occasion I must express my deep gratitude to Professor Dr. Kalidas Bhattacharyya, Professor of Philosophy, Visva-Bharati University, to whom I owe inspiration and guidance in undertaking this new line of investigation in an old field. I should further mention here, with due respect, the name of the late Mahamahopadhyaya Jogendranath Tarka-Vedantatirtha, D. Litt., once Research Professor of Indian Philosophy, Sanskrit College, Calcutta, who with loving care helped me for years to go through some of the difficult texts of Vedānta.

To my wife I owe a debt, though too personal, for her good judgment which has often helped me in finally preparing the manuscript.

In conclusion, I may just add, although some six years have passed since I wrote the thesis, I have now found little reason for any major and essential change in the work—although the late twenties and early thirties may well prove to be years of transformation for a growing mind. Subsequent first-hand studies in Phenomenology (during my two years of post-doctoral research in West Germany) have only confirmed my conviction that the phenomenological approach is suitable for interpreting afresh the basic Vedāntic standpoint of Subjectivity.

November, 1964. DEBABRATA SINHA

INTRODUCTION

There is a distinction between a metaphysics proper and what may be called a 'metaphysic of experience'. The former essentially signifies a theory of reality, a world-view deduced and speculatively constructed on the basis of some rationally evident principles. The latter, on the other hand, should be understood, if the said distinction is meaningfully drawn, as a critique of experience. Such analysis of experience in the first hand need not necessarily entail a system of metaphysics in the strict sense; or to put it in another way, it may stop short of a theory of reality as such. It could well be the case that a metaphysic of experience exhibit some definite direction towards a certain metaphysical belief. Similarly, an avowedly metaphysical endeavour could well proceed from or absorb analysis of experience which *per se* bore no sign of metaphysical commitment.

So this distinction—heuristic as it is—need not, in any case, resolve into polarities. On the contrary, they belong to the broad spectrum of what may otherwise be characterized as 'interpretation of experience'. Unlike metaphysics in the traditional speculative sense, what we prefer to call 'metaphysic of experience' seeks to interpret experience not in terms of a set of rationally conceived first principles or postulates, but with reference to the immanent structure of consciousness. Such perspective in broad would guide us in the attempt to meaningfully understand the central philosophy of the non-dualistic system of Vedānta—a system of critique of experience to be unfolded within its doctrine of 'Pure Consciousness' (*Cit*). The mode of interpretation introduced in this context seeks to proceed basically in terms of 'conditions for the possibility of experience', as Kant or Edmund Husserl (each in his respective context) might have stated. Neither naive belief nor theoretic presuppositions – whether on the factual or on the metaphysical level—could be accepted to interfere with the said analysis of experience.

Such investigation into the area of experience in the first hand need not, however, mean a barely psychological or anthropological enterprise. In both these disciplines the analysis of human experience is to be undertaken entirely in terms of the psycho-physical (psycho-biological-social too) complex that is human reality. A methodological suspension of belief in the natural and/or ontological reality would enclose the psychological-anthropological region too. The appropriate way to characterize this mode of philosophic reflexion is to call it 'transcendental' (in a broadly Kantian-phenomenological sense). Such characterization indicates a movement of reflexion from the level of empirically given to the ideal dimension of non-empirical non-natural 'essences' (as typically designated in phenomenology), which transcend yet ground the stratum of experience. The conditions for the possibility of experience—those that are themselves not empirically conditioned nor formally-axiomatically derived—are sought to be explored. This mode of description-cum-analysis, just briefly indicated here, may in effect be accepted as the one suitable for in-depth interpretation of experience without an *a priori* commitment to a *metaphysical* theory of Reality.

Coming to the matter of understanding the basic thesis of Advaita Vedānta, this is the approach that we principally seek to work out towards tracing in Vedānta a thorough exemplification of a system of critique of experience—at least in an implicit manner. It is, of course, true that the Advaita school of Vedānta, founded by Śaṅkara, and followed up, developed and ramified by post-Śaṅkara authors through the centuries (from 9th century A.D. onward), is generally represented as a full-fledged metaphysics of Being. Its uncompromising monistic doctrine is singularly focused on the concept of Absolute, that is Brahman, the all-engulfing Ultimate, which is itself unconditioned but to which all multiplicity whatsoever is sought to be reduced. Such monism, it is urged, proceeds basically from the logic of identity which is carried through in its vertical consistency. This monistic logic is further reinforced by a negative movement; the ultimate One is not just affirmed in its simple unity, but is further re-affirmed (indirectly and negatively) by way of the logic of non-difference (*abheda*). Thus arises a radical critique of difference (*bheda*), of duality (*dvaita*), of multiplicity (*nānātva*), of relations (*sambandha*) etc. Consequently follows a negative metaphysics of the world, a negative cosmology, which yet is not an outright negation or acosmism. For though never to be regarded as a 'second reality' (that is, besides Brahman), Advaita nevertheless grants a peculiarly intermediate ontic status to the empirical world as being neither existent nor non-existent but inexplicable (*aṅirvācya*).

All these may sound to be in line with rational metaphysics—that is, the thesis of Brahman (almost with a 'theological' overtone !) as the unconditioned indeterminate Absolute—a close ally to the 'Being' of Parmenides, or the 'Substance' of Spinoza. The logic of non-difference, again, with its tool of *bādha*, that is sublation or cancellation—a subsequent addition in Vedāntic thought—seems to be the right foundation for the Brahman-centric monistic edifice, with the magic wing of *Māyā*, that is phenomenally actual yet ontologically not real.

With this brief statement of the general metaphysical position of Vedānta, there could still arise a fundamental note of skepsis in our attempt at an interpretive understanding of its central doctrine. This pertains to the commonly stated Vedāntic thesis of *Sat-Cit*—that is, the principle of Being identified with that of Consciousness, or rather, pure Consciousness ('pure', of course, without any ethical undertone). It is the *Cit*-component in this supreme ontological equation—leaving aside in the present context the third component of *Ānanda*—which seems to present a special problem, if not a puzzlement, in this endeaour. The whole doctrine of *Sat* has been approached in the late post-Śaṅkara development of scholastic Vedānta largely in terms of formal arguments. But such a formalistically inclined treatment of the theme has more often than not undermined the characteristic significance of *Cit*, which has been so much in the focus of Vedāntic reflexions, right from the Upaniṣads. A mere abstract formulation of the principle of *Cit* in rational-metaphysical terms is apt to forgo its concrete bearing upon, and essential relevance to, the fabric of experience. What originally motivated Advaita as a *Cit*-centric philosophy is apt to be missed in a metaphysical equation which joins, more or less in conceptual hypostatisation, the generic essence of consciousness to the highest universal Being.

A far more illuminating way of approaching the Vedāntic theme of *Cit* should rather lie in demonstrating its total relevance to an in-depth critique of experience, proceeding right from the stratum of mundane human subjectivity or consciousness. So what is sought to be worked out in the following pages is an interpretation of experience oriented to the central focus of *cit*, that is pure consciousness. Indeed the very equivalence of the highest Reality with the essence of consciousness—*Sat* that is *Cit*—promotes a unique dimension to the Advaitic ontology, which would differentiate it from any other ontology of Being in the Western tradition, and perhaps most ontologies in the Eastern tradition too. Thus, in spite of the basic monism, the Vedāntic Being is unlike, for example, the Eleatic Being, or even the Spinozistic 'Substance'. This integral identity of *Sat* with *Cit* certainly demands an approach fundamentally different from an objectively (metaphysically) oriented conception of Being, where the latter is posited as in essence *other* than the knowing subject. So to rightly comprehend the Vedāntic thesis of *Sat-Cit*, we have to take the fullest cognizance of the unique significance of the notion of *cit*, and pose the thesis afresh in the light of the standpoint that could possibly yield a critique of experience oriented to a singular insight into the nature and essence of subjectivity.

Moving along this line of approaching the central Vedāntic thesis, we could as well envisage the possibility of introducing a perspective entirely from the other end of interpreting Śaṅkara in particular. In other words, instead of the exclusive emphasis on monism and illusionism (as a necessary corollary to the former), the focus might wholly be placed on the 'anthropological' concern in Śaṅkara—and in Advaita system in general. As at least one contemporary scholar has argued, Śaṅkara himself often reasoned about the self 'without employing any specifically monistic concept'.[1] The present context is not for introducing a discussion on the legitimacy of such a claim. Certainly Śaṅkara's original concern for the question of man, the human subject (*jīva*), who experiences, enjoys and suffers the involvement in the *Saṃsāra*, can hardly be overemphasized.

Yet to read the implicit philosophical anthropology standing out in the system as an unresolved component, not essentially integrated to its ontology at all, would not amount to a wholesome understanding of the Advaita doctrine in its authentic totality. What is to be recognised here is the essential integration, within the range of reflexion, of immanence and transcendence, of the empirical and the over-empirical. This is typically demonstrated in the two-way movement within the triad of *Brahman*, *jiva* and *Sākṣin**—Brahman being the uppermost limit and *Jiva* the lower limit forming the broad-spectrum conceptual-experiential polarity in the Advaita system.

In the otherwise ontologically loaded system of Vedānta, a scheme of experience-critique could be legitimized in terms of its own basic premises. We come across two major phases in the movement of Vedantic reflexion. Firstly, the Absolute, that is Brahman, is sought to be reduced from its transcendent height (the uppermost and outermost 'That'—*Tat*) to the region of immanent experience—reflection being directed to the subjective field of consciousness rather than to the metaphysical World-ground. Next there comes the stage of distinguishing the *pure* from the mundane factitive subjectivity; that would imply the restoring of the true (innermost) essence of subjectivity behind the complex of empirical consciousness as marked by the individual self in the form of 'I-subject' (*ahamātmā*).[2] An analysis of consciousness that could broadly be characterized as 'phenomenological' pertains evidently to the latter phase of the said enterprise (as to be shown in the sequel).

Now to come back to the proposed methodological approach, already indicated as 'transcendental.' It has to be differentiated from (though not exactly opposed to) the bare formal-logical method so often treated as essential to metaphysical thinking. That is, the former approach cannot be identified with the steps of deduction from what are acknowledged to be universal *a priori* principles, holding good as rational and self-evident. Nor does it imply an ontological commitment to the reality

*The cardinal concept of *sākṣin*, that is 'witness' or 'witnessing consciousness', is introduced and explored later in our investigation.

of empirical existence (other than its bare empiricality). In other words, both the naive natural attitude towards things, as well as the metaphysical attitude of constructing, hypostatising and deducing in a formal *a priori* fashion, are 'out of play' (as Husserl, for example, might have put it).

In the light of such approach, which need not exclusively be identified with any particular philosophical system as such, it follows that an *a priori* assertion regarding ultimate Reality has to be suspended—or for that matter, any formal-rational statement pertaining to the supposed structure of Reality. Principles, on the other hand, are to be posited, or realities affirmed, according as consciousness *means* or refers to them. No external criterion, empirical or ratiocinative, other than what the cognizing—and for that matter, meaning—consciousness refers to, should be introduced, if a systematic critique of experience is introduced in a non-dogmatic manner. The characteristic (idealist, in a special sense) position of Advaita Vedānta in a way exemplifies such an approach, in its significant (epistemological) formulation that the nature of the object is determined in accordance with the way it is presented to consciousness (which means or refers to it) "*yathā saṃvid-avabhāsādhinatvāt arthasattāniścaya.*"[3]

So the relevant mode of consciousness, as referring to what is presented to it, rather than any 'objective' standard, entailing in the long run a metaphysics of the object *per se*, should prove to be the arbiter of validity in an in-depth reflective procedure. But in such approach, it might be pointed out, the entire accent is put on the subject's knowing rather than on the object known (or to be known). The point of view of the cognising (experiencing, to put it in broader terms) subject is put forward in preference to that of the object; and such reversal of the object-ward attitude may seem to be *prima facie* unwarranted, if not unnatural. The ground, however, for a subject-centric attitude—if the said attitude could be so characteized, to contra-distinguish it from the object-centric or objective attitude—need not be far to seek. At this stage it might just be pointed out that the legitimacy of a subject-ward attitude in philosophic reflexion could at least be drawn from a bare recognition of some uniqueness about the notion of human subject *qua* subject, as plainly conveyed by the expression 'I'. The objective attitude, commonly affirmed or practised, need not be the only attitude in philosophy—a point which would be more explicit as we proceed in our investigations.

This, however, would perhaps bring up further the question: what would, then, be the attitude towards the question of *real* object ? Does the proposed approach have any explanation of *objectivity* to offer ? It seems to be evident that in a possible critique of experience, as envisaged here, the focus is shifted from the object *per se*, supposed to be real independent of noetic reference, to 'objectivity'. The latter indicates the way of givenness of the object as meant by the knowing-experiencing subject. Consequently, the common charge that the subject-centric position necessarily ignores objective givenness, and as such gives no explanation of the world of objective experience, need not hold good—unless, of course, subjectivism is taken in the sense of mentalistic reductionism of some kind.

On the other hand even with a commitment to such 'subjective' point of view, the minimum tenet of realism (or rather empirical realism) need not be given up. For all practical purpose, the independent reality of empirical world of things and beings cannot be denied. In fact, Advaita generally contends in favour of a pragmatic (*vyāvahārika*) status or validity of the world of common experience. On the other hand, any psychological determination of objective reality in terms of contents in the minds of actual psychophysical ego, is resisted in that philosophy. So our proposed approach, by way of inner look at consciousness with its modes of referentiality, is not supposed to involve any 'psychologistic' position at all.

Now, in Advaita Vedānta we do not, strictly speaking, meet with apriorism in the same way as one would find in European philosophy—right from Plato down to phenomenology, though in a wide range of variations of the specific meaning and use of the concept of *a priori*. As a matter of fact, it could be said in respect of Indian philosophy in general (except perhaps, in a certain sense, the Vaiyākaraṇas or the philosophers of Grammar) that it does not have a place for the *a priori* in the strict sense of universality and necessity, with all its epistemological-metaphysical implications. So Vedānta would not proceed in terms of the logical structure of thought *mutatis mutandis* the structure of Reality. (As it may come out in the sequel, we could meaningfully talk of the structure of *appearance*, in the context of a possibly constructed *avidyā*-oriented metaphysic of experience).

However, such apriorism apart, Vedānta could still be considered in the light of what has already been referred to as a 'transcendental' approach.* The latter here means the understanding of an overtly metaphysical system of transcendent Reality in terms of the conditions for the possibility of experience, without necesary reference to metaphysical presuppositions or beliefs. To that extent Vedānta is sought to be viewed as a kind of 'descriptive metaphysics', although with a "revisionary" motive —to borrow P.F. Strawson's distinction (cf. *Individuals*), without, of course, following his line of ordinary language analysis. In the Vedāntic context, however, unlike in the phenomenological philosophy of the West, the central concern is focused on the human condition, rather than on theoretic-scientific explorations of the modes of objectivity or of the structures of idealities. Some structure of appearance or objectivity could possibly be traced within the frame of reference of its experience-critique; but whatever picture follows is to be derived from its basic doctrine of *Cit*. As Śaṅkara states the central concern of Vedānta right at the outset of his commentary on the Brahma Sūtra : all Vedānta is directed towards establishing the doctrine of oneness and integrity of Self (*ātmaikatva*), with a view to dispelling the root cause of all the delusive disvalue (*anartha*) overcoming the individual (*jiva*).[4]

As the basis of such an approach to Vedānta, however, lies the standpoint of subjectivity, in a special sense—or to be more explicit, transcendental subjectivity. The central idealist standpoint ('idealism', again, is not to be understood in this context in the usual metaphysical sense) of Advaita Vedānta is to be identified with the cardinal principle of *Cit*. The latter, with all its trans-subjetive ontological status recognised in the Advaita system, does still represent the very essence of human

*The term 'transcendental' (rather than 'transcendent') has been used in this broadly Kantian-cum-phenomenological sense (epistemologically oriented, metaphysically non-committal) throughout the book.

subjectivity (as our study attempts to show in the following chapters). As such, *cit* indicates the paradigm *par excellence*, in terms of which the meaning of subjectivity could be comprehended and at the same time the standpoint for exploring and analysing the structure of experience in depth ensured.

A broadly phenomenological approach—may not be in the strictly Husserlian sense—could thus possibly provide the interpretive understanding of a philosophical doctrine without necessary reference to the metaphysical or like presuppositions that might otherwise be involved in the system concerned. To consider the doctrine of *Cit*, playing the role of transcendental subjectivity within a possible system of critique of experience, broadly phenomenological lines of interpretation can legitimately be introduced—to what extent and fulfilment shall be seen in the sequel.

Yet, methodological considerations apart, the essentially *ontological* orientation of *Cit* or pure consciousness *qua* transcendental subjectivity in the scheme of Advaitic metaphysic of experience, could hardly be overlooked. The Vedāntic *Cit* is indeed indicated as the principle of pure consciousness, which is at the same time ontological existence or Being. However, at least heuristically, we propose to project *Cit* in terms of its phenomenological focus, keeping the ontological-metaphysical dimensions in abeyance. Thus viewed, *Cit* promises the possible foundation and background for what otherwise could be accepted as the epistemological, psychological and anthropological investigations within the system of Advaita Vedānta. To that extent we can legitimately speak of the unique role of *cit* in a possible system of critique of experience—one that can legitimately be interpreted as the 'transcendental' role.

NOTES AND REFERENCES

1. See Paul Hacker, "A Note on Śaṅkara's Conception of Man" in *German Scholars on India : Cantributions to Indian Studies*, Vol. I. Varanasi, 1973 (p. 100).

Also Hacker's article, "Sankara der Yogin und Sankara der Advaitin : einige Beobachtungen" in : Festschrift fur E. Frauwallner, *Wiener Zeitschrift fur die Kunde Sud-und Ostasiens*, Vol. 12/13, 1968.

2. Cf. "Brahmaṇaḥ parokṣasya pratyakṣatvasiddhyaye ahamātmatvam upadiśya punaḥ tadvyudāsena mukhyātmatvam upadiśati", *Pañcapādikā-Vivaraṇa* (subsequently referred to as *Vivaraṇa*), *Varṇaka* I (p. 57f.)

3. *Vivaraṇa* I (p. 21).

4. Cf. "asya anarthahetoḥ prahāṇāya ātmaikatvavidyā-pratipattaye sarve vedāntā ārabhyante", *Brahma-Sūtra Śāṅkara-Bhāṣya, Adhyāsa-bhāṣya* (*Upodghāta*).

PART ONE

THE CONCEPTION OF PURE CONSCIOUSNESS (*CIT*)

Chapter I

APPROACH TO *CIT* QUA SUBJECTIVITY

The possible way of approaching *Cit* in the Advaita doctrine, apart from its metaphysical thesis, would be to understand it in the light of a transcendental analysis of experience. The ground for such approach may not be far to seek. For, consciousness *prima facie* stands for what can roughly be called the subjective, or simply be characterized—though negatively—as being other than the object in the epistemic situation. And *cit*, to have a definite import other than the metaphysical, should rather be defined in terms of the subjective. So our major problem here would be to show how far *cit* can, and does, claim to stand as the presuppositional ground in the subjectively oriented interpretation of experience. It is to the definition and elaboration of the notion of *cit* as having the unique import of subjectivity that the chapters in Part One are directed.

It is to be noted in this connexion that our enquiry would centre not around the subject that is *metaphysically* real, but rather towards the supposed foundational essence involved within the range of experience taken as *meant*. Accordingly, the procedure may be viewed not in terms of existence, natural or ontological, but in terms of transcendental preconditions of experience. With a view to bringing out the foundational status of consciousness, relevant logico-epistemological and psychological analyses, largely in keeping with Advaita philosophy, would be undertaken. Nevertheless, the attitude in broad of bringing in no metaphysical presupposition as such is sought to be maintained, so that a proper criticism of experience in the light of what Kant would call 'transcendental reflection'* may follow.

*　　　　*　　　　*

*For the actual bearing of 'transcendental reflection' (as distinguished from 'logical reflection' by Kant), vide Ch. V.

To begin with an epistemological enquiry, what seems to be accepted is nothing more nor less than the undeniable rudimentary fact to which all individual cognition may be reduced, namely, 'I know'. Consciousness, although about something, stands nonetheless *for* the subject. For some, notably the Naiyāyikas, to speak of the *subjective* character of consciousness would mean that it necessarily pertains to a subject who knows or experiences as distinguished from the object experienced or known. But the genuine subjectivity of consciousness seems to lie deeper. For fitstly, though Nyāya holds that consciousness belongs to a self, this self may remain without it; secondly, the so-called 'subjective' of the Naiyāyika proves on further analysis to be as much objective as other things.

The true subjectivity intrinsic to consciousness would mean a different position and has to be shown differently. The principle of *cit* in Advaita doctrine indicates consciousness not as attributive and empirical but as transcendentally substantive. Consciousness *prima facie* would mean phenomena which are generally considered subjective, i.e., those which pertain to the subject (experiencer or knower). But to contend that consciousness in essence is subjectivity implies at once two steps. (1) Consciousness is not what just appears in the shape of conscious states in individual minds empirically determined but rather what presuppositionally stands behind such states. (2) The alleged core of consciousness should be such as to subsist by itself independent of extrinsic factors—objective or psychological. And this would signify its possible autonomy, i.e., its subsistence independent of empirical determination and objective reference.

Both these steps, however, imply the *prima facie* possibility of considering consciousness to be a distinct principle at all. There are thinkers who would hardly admit consciousness to be a distinct principle. Consciousness, they urge, can never be posited apart from the empirical context. As empiricists they would contend that consciousness as distinct is hardly to be found. Hume, for instance, would rather reduce self to 'bundle of perceptions' and as such deny outright any substantive status to it as subject.

Now, the first step in showing the possiblity of self-subsisting consciousness would necessitate an analysis of knowledge-relation itself. To regard knowledge-relation simply as objectively (causally) determined, as a realist would have it, is to miss the *raison d'etre* of knowledge itself. Even for a realist, who takes knowledge-relation like *any* relation between two facts, knowledge is regarded as a simple fact not further analysable. However, to admit knowledge-relation as simple fact like any objective event would little improve our genuine understanding of knowledge. This may prompt us to a reversal of the attitude in which the object is cognised. That would mean stressing the subjective side rather than that of the object. Accordingly, the peculiar feature of 'reference' as pertaining to knowledge has to be recognised. To consider the epistemological import of the knowledge-of-object situation, the simple proposition 'This is X' may give place to a more reflective proposition 'I have the knowledge of X'. And in the latter proposition, the 'of'-ness implies that there is a reference to X. To posit an object amounts invariably to a directedness on the part of the cognising subject. Thus each instance of cognition is the cognition of something. The directedness towards something other than the knowing consciousness itself is indicated by the reference character of knowledge (or what the phenomenologists would call "intentionality").*

As between knowledge and object, it is with the former as subjective act that we find the peculiar referencehood. For in stating the knowledge-of-object situation, the 'of'-ness, is meant to belong to the knowing act rather than to the objects. If, however, the situation be put in terms of 'object-of-knowledge', then the latter would mean the object-as-known; this in other words means that *knownness* (*jñātatā*) belongs to the object. But what is the status of this so-called 'knownness' in relation to the object?**

*The typical phenomenological treatment of consciousness rests on the unique feature of 'intentionality' (originally advocated by Brentano); that every 'cogito' must be consciousness *of* something is to be interpreted not simply as a psychological fact.

**For detailed analysis of 'knownness', vide infra, Sec. A.

Even if it be granted that knownness is a character belonging to object, its distinction from other objective qualities like colour, taste, smell etc. has still to be admitted. While the latter cannot be considered apart from the object as the locus, knownness cannot be so considered. Certain objective qualities like spatiality, nay even sound etc., may as well be treated apart from objective configurations and thereby ensuring, for instance, Geometry as the science of Space or Acoustics as the science of Sound. But such separate treatment is enabled only through mechanical abstraction of the qualities concerned from the composite structure of things. The unique character of knownness, on the other hand, presents itself as capable of being treated as such. This can explain why Psychology could at all proceed with the conscious phenomenon of knownness (and of felt-ness and willed-ness, to that extent) more or less independently of the objective (bodily) counterpart. Moreover, knownness presupposes the act of knowing as somehow outside the bounds of the object itself. As such, it can hardly be regarded as the original character of the object. On the contrary, while knowledge refers to the object, the latter does not intrinsically refer to consciousness.

Referencehood thus belongs inseparably to the subject-pole. When A refers to B, it follows that B is here to be understood necessarily in the context of A's reference (although it need not at once follow that B has *per se* no existential status of its own). So far as B is sought to be explained in terms of A's act, that A may subsist independent of B suggests itself to us. It follows that A should presumably have a self-subsistent autonomous nature of its own apart from its actual reference to B, which means A subsisting independent of the B-context.

The train of analysis suggested above would in broad agree with the fundamental idealistic position of Advaita as noted earlier. To come to the thesis of the autonomous status of consciousness, Advaita seeks to trace pure consciousness in the background of cognitive states. Any state of consciousness (*vṛtti*) is on reflective analysis found to be involving the common element of consciousness. The varying cognitive states, having different objects from case to case, invariably share the common character of knowingness (*jñānatva*). This character of knowingness as generic is felt to be not merely associated but identified with the states themselves; but it is not nominally posited as on the strength of mere abstraction. It is due to fusion with the varying modifications that the generic character itself appears to be varying. For the character of pure knowingness is, on the last analysis, the manifestation of the object to the knowing subject; and this character in its turn abides in the self.* Now, such generic character as approached through conscious states points to the concrete possibility of consciousness as self-subsisting essence. Of course, such concrete essence may not be realised in actuality apart from the media of psychic states partaking of the generic character. To pass from the generic character (*sāmānya*) to the concrete embodiment of the generic essence —*vyakti*, not *jāti* or class—seems to be a typically significant procedure of Advaita. What is envisaged as the generic essence bears the *possibility* that such essence may be concretely embodied.[1]

Now, knowingness is not to be looked upon as a property of mental states like other properties such as causality, numericality, succession etc. The latter may pertain to the contents of mind but are not conceivable apart from the context of the contents themselves. Knowingness in general, however, can be conceived by itself independent of its belonging to any specific states. In this also the autonomy of knowingness is suggested.

Consciousness as it appears obviously varies in *form* from one state to another, so that the *essential* consciousness, alleged to be common to the various apparent forms of consciousness, may well be questioned. But the apparent differences in form may be resolved in the light of the referential aspect of consciousness and traced to the object-counterpart of the states of consciousness concerned. So far as the pure ground behind the states is concerned, it should not be conceived of as partaking of any form of objective reference varying according to the given object—although the ground itself is *ideally* posited rather than actually realised.[2]

---

*For the Advaitic equation of consciousness and knowledge (*cit* as *jñāna*), or the interpretation of the essence of consciousness in purely cognitive terms, vide infra, Ch. II.

From this preliminary survey pure consciousness (*Cit*) as self-subsistent subjectivity comes out at least as a *possibility*. With a view to strengthening this possibility by demonstraing the ontic validity of consciousness as the essential subjectivity, we now proceed to the detailed consideration of certain approaches as can be worked out in the context of the Advaita metaphysic of experience. Besides the so-called phenomenon of knownness, an analysis of the three-fold stages of experience in the forms of waking, dream and deep sleep and also the notion of 'I' would provide for Advaita several approaches to the notion of *Cit* as pure subjectivity.

Section A. Analysis of Knownness (*jñātatā*)

A closer examination of the epistemological character of knownness (besides what have been said in the preliminary remarks) would bring into view in the present context the treatment of the concept in the Bhāṭṭa school of Mīmāṃsā. According to the Bhāṭṭas, knownness (*jñātatā*)or manifestness (*prākaṭya*) is a character pertaining to the object, indicating the relation of self or subject to the object known. As knowledge is generated, the relation between the object and the knower is grasped. In an instance of knowledge as stated in the judgment, "This is known by me", the object referred to rather than the the subject, is primarily apprehended. This apparent primacy of the objective factor over the subjective is to be attributed to this relation between the object and the knower.

Now this character of knownness, resulting through knowledge-relation, is taken to be inhering in the object of knowledge in context as inseparable therefrom and is to be grasped through sense-perception along with the object. As this knownness is apprehended, it serves as the sign on the ground of which knowledge is inferred as the cause of such a quality as knownness—*jñātatāliṅgānuamāna.* So the object being known, the knowledge itself is known subsequently through inference.[3] As Pārthasārathi Miśra point out, knowledge is to be postulated as the adventitious cause which brings about the connection of the self with the object.[4]

It seems that the new quality of knownness should belong to the object known rather than the subject knowing, though the contrary view is not missing among the Bhāṭṭa thinkers. According to Vācaspati Miśra's interpretation ("*Nyāyakaṇikā*"), the quality of knownness should inhere in the self and as such be amenable to internal perception (*mānasa pratyakṣa*). Knownness, however, is kept apart from knowledge, so far as the former is obtained through mental perception, while the latter through inference. But this would entail an unnecessary dichotomy between knownness and knowledge, both abiding in the self. Knownness as located in the self could bear meaning only in the sense of reference of knowledge to object; and it is exactly this reference that is involved in knowledge as the *tertium quid* between self and object.

So the only alternative admissible seems to be to take knownness, pertaining to object, as the quality effected by knowledge — a position mentioned by Pārthasārathi and accepted generally by later Bhāṭṭas. Knowledge itself has its own character (*jñānatvam*) and the knower its own (*jñātṛtvam*); so knownness should naturally belong to the object known. But the question may still be raised: how from knownness, a character admittedly objective or at least pseudo-objective, can the subjective principle like knowledge be inferred ? For, the Bhāṭṭas do admit that knowledge, unlike knownness, is after all a quality in the self rather than in the object. Further it is maintained that knownness is an added quality to the object. But to recognize such addition (*atiśaya*) as due to the activity of knowing would entail that the latter has somehow been apprehended, whether prior to or simultaneous with the object. Without the knowledge being apprehended, it would be rather presumptuous to accept 'knownness' merely on the basis of such judgment as 'The pot is known' (put in a more explicit but sophisticated way as 'Knownness belongs to the pot')

Again, the very process of inferring knowledge in the Bhāṭṭa way would involve difficulties. In order to infer knowledge, knownness as the ground (*hetu*) is supposed to be cognised. How, then, to cognise knownness itself ? The simple answer may be, as some Bhāṭṭa thinkers hold: through perception of knownness along with the object. But if knownness can be directly grasped, why not knowledge itself be similarly apprehended — which would, of course, mean surrendering the Bhāṭṭa position ?

Moreover in such a view, knownness would be reduced to one of the objective qualities—a contention already examined. On the other hand, from a consistent Bhāṭṭa approach it would follow that knownness, if itself known, should entail secondary knownness, and that in its turn a tertiary one, and so and on. Thus an indefinite series of 'knownnesses' should follow, so that to infer knowledge on the basis of knownness (as known) would prove to be a baffling task.

A naively objective approach seems to escape the question of knowledge (as such) over and above the object. But in that case, no reference to knownness could be made at all, nor to knowledge besides the object in view. As soon as the question of knowledge by way of knownness be raised, the absurd regress of 'knownness' would be inescapable. So, the apprehension of knownness as an objective quality would be unjustified. To treat knownness as a quality in the object, with which the supposed knowledge bears a contingent relation, implies only an improper abstraction. Even accepting for the sake of argument that knownness is *prima facie* an objective quality, a reflective analysis reveals its unique character as transcending the context of the object into the subjective act of knowing. The very absurdity of interpreting knownness in objective terms points to the originally unobjective level of knowledge—in other words, the level of subjectivity.

Section B. Notion of I or Ego (*Ahaṅkāra*)

An investigation into the notion of I-hood or egoity (*ahaṅkāra*) can also provide a way of demonstrating *cit* as the foundational subjectivity. The individual is indicated by 'I' and as such I-hood is taken to stand for individuality (the latter broadly meant to include mind or internal organ). So far as the notion of 'I' at least *prima facie* involues the element of consciousness, a search for the essence of I-hood should lead to *cit* as the essence of subjectivity.

An ambiguity seems, however, to be involved in the very notion of *individuality* itself. For, the individuality as embodied in 'I' should be distinguished from the individuality of things such as a tree, a rock etc. And the point of distinction apparently lies in the presence in the one and the absence in the other of the element of subjectivity. What seems to be common to both the types of individuals—*I* as well as the tree—is apparently the factor of self-contained identity. But the unique feature of individual subject is that it contains within itself the element of self-distinguishment which may be regarded as the mark of its subjectivity. The subject alone is denoted by 'I', and not the things. In the case of objective entities I-ness is missing. The position of personal pronouns other than the first, viz. 'you', 'he' etc. may be characterized as quasisubjective. For though they do not *actually* denote 'I' they can neither be identified with the object-individual; the possibility of being represented by 'I' from *their* respective points of view (though not that of the speaker) cannot, after all, be denied.

To put it schematically, at the one end of the hierarchy of individuality stands bare individuality (of things)*minus* subjectivity, while at the other end subsists—at least ideally—pure subjectivity devoid of individuality. At the intermediate stage (or stages) alone, one may find amalgamation, in varying proportions, of the elements of both individuality and subjectivity. It is in this region that the subject-individual may prevail. So, both the elements of individuality and of subjectivity are combined in the entity usually denoted by 'I'. In such combination however, one of the elements need not imply the other (in a more or less Hegelian way) as dialectically involved within itself; rather, even if co-existent, two elements are separable. That the two are at least primarily separate is suggested by the evidence of object-individual, where the element of bare individuality seems to prevail. This by itself at least suggests a possibility that subjectivity could subsist at the other end apart from individuality.

We next come upon a distinction of levels—reflective and unreflective—as may be traced in the I-consciousness. I-hood in its unreflective phase indicates the bodily level, where I as such and the feeling of *I* are not distinguished from each other. In this region of empirical use (*vyavahāra*), all that prevails is a bare feeling of *I*-ness, without the *I*-character being distinguished, enabling the common use in respect of self as body. Such functional appearance of *I*, however, may provide the point of departure for the search after pure *I*.

Śaṅkara—and idealists may generally agree with him in this respect—takes body-self identity (*dehātmatā*) to be a case of false identification(*adhyāsa*). They have thereby in view the reflective *I*, claiming to be distinct from the bodily complex. Such bodily level of individuality, where self is fused with the body, has been admitted by the Naiyāyika realist too to be false. Reflection on the body-self identity may bring home the notion of self as such. But, for the uncompromising naturalist like Cārvāka, the level of bodily self is the final stage which need not and cannot be transcended. At best there are shades of naturalism, taking self variously as the gross body (*sthūlaśarira*) or as sense-organs or as vital principle (*Prāṇa*) or even as mind (*manas*), taken roughly as the'subtle body' (*sūkṣma śarira*). From such statements in use as (a) 'I' am stout', (b) 'I am deaf', (c) 'I am thirsty', (d) 'I am with doubt', the characterizations in terms of body, sense-organ, vital principle and mind respectively are transferred to self.[5] But these are, after all, stages in approaching the pure self—beginning with the primary level of belief in the bodily self. That we can hardly confine ourselves finally to these stages may be shown as we come to the reflective analysis of I-consciousness.

I or ego at the reflective level is recognised as the inner principle distinct from the bodily complex. Such a principle, though having reference to body, still claims to be distinct. However, Advaita aptly recognises the intimate relation that exists between body and self. Here it comes remarkably close to the contention of some modern thinkers (like S. Alexander), who would hold—on the basis of adequate knowledge of the relation between the body and mental functions—that not only is mind vaguely connected with body but there is an intimate connection which does not enable us to rest in the conception of their mutual independence.[6] Advaita would not take the body-self identification as merely gratuitous or nominal; it is basic, because the identity is actually felt.

Here comes into view the distinction between mediate knowledge and immediate perception in respect of the I-notion. So far as our perception is concerned, *I* is hardly to be apprehended except in its connection with the bodily complex. On the perceptual level, the self presents itself ordinarily in the context of the causal chain of bodily activities (*kārya-kāraṇa-saṅghāta*), and not as distinct from the latter. Through rational reflection alone is self known to be possibly distinct. Such evident fact that the same *I* is felt to persist from childhood, while the body undergoes organic changes from time to time, serves as the ground for inferring that the ego-substance (*ahampadārtha*) as denoted by *I* must possibly be distinct in essence from the bodily complex.[7] In another way Śaṅkara shows the distinctness of self from body. Starting from the common-sense position that self, even as the knower of all sense-manifold, is necessarily confined to the bodily complex, he further points out that body is itself knowable (*jñeya*). So, if self is taken as nothing more than body, it would mean that one knowable is known by another knowable, which implies an evident absurdity. Through this ***reductio ad absurdum*** Śaṅkara maintains the trans-bodily character of self.[8]

Still, the primary sense of body-self identity can never be regarded as merely verbal, because such identity comes to us as a fact of perception. Even through critical reflection, *I* as dissociated from the bodily complex is not *actually* realized, though through such reflection alone the pure *I* can be envisaged. But the sense of body-self identity on the perceptual level can be superseded not through inference but through the higher level of 'intuition' of the true nature of self.

The bodily association—even if taken as necessary—does not preclude the trans-bodily character of the ego; the element of subjectivity does make itself felt within the I-notion. According to Alexander, the self as 'person' is to be considered as 'the synthesis of the self as subject and the self as body or as object'.[9] In spite of his attempt to reduce the subject to 'a development of the bodily self', he would still admit the unique character of the subjective element as not quite amenable to objective experience. (Of course, Alexander's final definition of subjectivity need not be accepted here.) Again, the apparent uniqueness about the I-notion is admitted by Ryle—*I* unlike any other pronoun being never exhaustively grasped, though always felt to be proximate.[10] The point, however, remains whether apart from the said "systematic elusiveness", there is any *positive* essence about *I*. The Advaita position in this regard would be quite unambiguous. Subjectivity is felt from the very beginning in I-notion. As Śaṅkara remarks (*Adhyāsabhāṣya*), by virtue of immediacy (*aparokṣatva*), the innermost self (*pratyagātmā*) makes itself evident with indubitable certainty. In Vācaspati's definition of *Pratyagātmā*, inner subjectivity is characterised by unique definiteness as distinct from the indefiniteness about our feeling of body, sense-organs etc.[11]

Now the question is : if self is in essence *unobjective* (*aviṣaya*), as Vedānta insists, how could it be the object of I-notion (*asmatpratyayaviṣaya*) ? Such apparent logical absurdity is explained in Advaita by recourse to the principle of nescience (*avidyā*). The general principle apart, what is unobjective in essence assumes objectivity, even if apparent, through associational conditions (*upādhi*). As a result, the familiar phenomenon of ego is there—presenting a peculiar blend of the essential element of consciousness and the inessential non-conscious (*acit*) element. Ego appears determinable only in respect of the non-conscious element definable in terms of 'this' (*idam*). What eludes determination in terms of 'this'—*anidam*—is the element of consciousness (*cit*). Thus ego is conceived as partaking of the dual character of 'this' and 'not-this' (*idamanidamrūpa*)[12] It thus marks for Advaita the significant stage where the actual and the ideal meet. Śaṅkara virtually accepts the principle of egoity (*ahaṅkāra*) as the first step of inexplicable fusion (*tādātmya*) between pure subjectivity and the objective, wherefrom the whole series of empirical-psychological categories—those of agency (*kartṛtva*), enjoyership (*bhokṛtva*) and so on—follow. Here is the nodal point, as it were, binding together consciousness and the non-conscious—*cidacidgranthi*.[13]

Thus we understand how self, in spite of its unobjective certitude, comes to be the object of I-notion through the principle of egoity. Pure subjectivity assumes the character of *ahaṅkāra*, when reflected on the internal organ (*antaḥkaraṇa*) and getting fused with it.[14] According to *Vivaraṇa*, the evidencing consciousness which remains in the baekground assumes the explicit character of I-hood through reflection on the 'transparent' medium of *antaḥkaraṇa*.[15] The I-principle is unique in marking the common meeting point for the knower and the known alike. From this fact of coincidence of the two (in such a statemant as 'I know myself'), the Bhāṭṭa thinker goes to ascribe inertness to self in its 'known' aspect. Apart from the difficulties in admitting partial inertness of self, Advaita would put the burden of such amalgamation on the ego-principle. The knowable object-element in egoity is accounted for with reference to *antaḥkaraṇa*. Again, subjectivity—seated in egoity and yet tending to transcend it—cannot be regarded as involving within itself the dual elements of subject and object, for that would only mar its native homogeneity. So, while self is not equated with ego, the latter in its turn cannot be reduced to an inert principle.*

Rational reflection would posit consciousness as distinct from, and beyond the stage of, egoity. Consequently, the appearance of pure subject as the object of I-notion has to be treated as false on deeper analysis. And this is meant when I-notion is taken to be a case of 'secondary reference' (*gauṇī vṛtti*), by way of which the self that is as such unobjective comes to be objective in use.[16]

As shown so far, between the two ends of object and subject—both in their own ways devoid of I-hood—the intermediate stage of actual I-hood prevails. Commonly we move within the range of this stage, presenting shades of identity (*tādātmya*) between pure subjectivity and the physico-mental correlates and pervaded in general by the I-sense. Thus, on the bodily level, for instance, besides the perception of 'I-body' (or I as body), such perception as '*my* body' may also prevail. In the latter case, unlike in the former, the body is felt somehow as distinct from self, while the latter is likewise felt *qua* its capacity for possessing the body. In the one, *I* is wholly identified with body and in the other, it is felt as distinct and yet bound up with the latter. On the mental level, a distinction as between 'I-mind' (i.e., I am the mind)

---

*For a further phenomenological treatment of *Cit vis-a-vis ahaṅkāra* and detailed analysis of the relevant stages, vide infra, Chap. VI.

and '*my* mind' would similarly prevail. Broadly in this way, the pure *I* may gradually be approached in degrees of subjectivity, with corresponding dissociation from physico-mental complex. The possibility of pursuing *I* in such steps of dissociation—right from the bodily level—suggests the possibility of pure *I* as beyond the bodily complex, nay even beyond the mental manifold. And as the process is contrary to being object-ward the essence that may *ideally* be posited at the end is naturally to be conceived as *unobjective*.

However, granting pure subjectivity to be *ideally free from* physico-mental associations, it is yet hard to conceive of such supposed subjectivity to be devoid of individuality altogether. A completely de-individualised subject seems *prima facie* to be almost an anachronism.* Without going into the mooted question as to how far, on ultimate analysis, individuality can be retained in pure subjectivity, one point may here be emphasized. The stage of pure subjectivity should mark the termination, ideally though it may be, of progressive subjectivisation—a process which need not be accompanied by a corresponding effacement of the *I*-sense. It may rather be called a case of 'rarefaction' than of complete 'evaporation' of the I-feeling, with which we start—a position which, nevertheless, may not be endorsed by the traditional Advaita view.

Section C. Evidence Of Deep Sleep (*suṣupti*)

Our ordinary experience is marked by two distinct stages of waking and dream. And an empirical-psychological account as such would hardly go beyond these states. The stage of sleep as devoid of dream, if admitted, would have little importance for it except as supporting in indirect way the continuity of the psychological self or 'stream of consciousness or of subjective life' (W. James).[17] In this respect we mark in Advaita a point of departure from ordinary psychology. In Advaita (as also in Yoga system), three distinct stages of waking, dream and sleep are recognised in marked distinctness. The recognition of a new dimension in the state

*The point here and the one in the previous paragraph will be more elaborately discussed later in course of our discourse.

of dreamless sleep (*suṣupti*) is a significant addition to ordinary psychology. In order to comprehend the proper import of this new dimension, we should proceed from waking to dream and from dream to deep sleep—marking the steps of withdrawal from objective experience.

In the waking state, sensations directly refer to things or objects. Even in mental constructions, finding place in the said state, the presentative element plays the dominant role. In dream, on the other hand, all that we have are mainly copies of waking experience rather than presentative percepts themselves. Moreover, imaginative construction, though obscure, has a freer play in dream; while in waking life the possibility of combination and association in terms of ideas is conditioned and controlled by the demand of practical interest and empirical belief. Further, in dream unlike in waking, the limiting sense of body as the constant centre of reference is reduced to a minimum—with consequent freedom among dream-contents.[18] Dream has thus to be approached in the light of a gradual lapse of waking consciousness. The object of dream-awareness remains more or less in an ideal form, devoid of spatial and temporal determinations and free from the sense of objective continuity. As to the question of *reality* of dream-contents, Śaṅkara points out that dream-phenomena lack the attributes of reality, viz., spatiality, temporality, causality and non-contradiction (*deśakālanimitta-sampattirabādhaśca*).[19] The illusoriness of dream experience would consequently follow (*māyāmātram svapnadarśanam*).[20] The qualitative distinction of dream in relation to waking lies not in respect of consciousness as such but of the character of dream-contents differing from objects of waking experience.

Now, the state of deep sleep may primarily be understood simply as the state of complete rest for the individual mind, exhausted through waking and dream experience. At this stage where even dreams do not prevail, psychic states seem to cease functioning altogether—sense-organs remaining inactive. The associational as well as the apperceptive aspects of mind seem to be conspicuous by their absence. One misses even the sense of *I* which recurs subsequently. In short, it is a seeming blankness in experience. But Advaita does not rest with a superficial account of such a typical case of experience. It rather seeks to find out the background of memory occurring in the waking state. Such memory, however vague, seems to refer to the experience of 'not knowing anything'. And this feeling of ignorance cannot certainly be ascribed to the dream state either, as the latter is not devoid of contents.

From the common-sense point of view, however, it may be urged that the alleged absence of knowledge is simply to be inferred from a comparison of the memory of pre-sleep state with the perception of post-sleep state. But a careful verdict of experience following upon deep sleep may be different. Thus the evidence of such judgments as 'I slept blissfully and I did not know anything' has to be closely analysed. To consider the latter part of the judgment viz., 'I did not know anything', it is broadly speaking yielded through introspection so far as it records internal psychic state and no external event. Moreover, a reference, however indistinct, to past stage gives it a semblance of memory—though we need not take it as an ordinary case of memory. For the memory of *negative* facts, external or internal, should be treated as different from that of positive mental states or of external objects.*

The situation may be approached in the light of the cognition of absence-of-a-particular-object. The prior absence (*prāgabhāva*) of a thing is said to be felt or perceived in the locus concerned. The very recognition of the previous absence of the self-same thing in the given locus would imply that the actual absence of the same in the locus concerned must have been somehow noticed while the former had not been there. Thus it is the present perception of past absence which necessitates, as it were, that the actual absence were similarly perceived. In this sense of perception of objective fact, we might speak of 'knowledge of absence as a present fact' (as K.C. Bhattacharya in *The Subject as Freedom*, Ch. IV does).

---

*Of course, Advaita commonly holds it to be a plain case of memory (*smṛti*)—a contention which however need not as such be accepted. Accordingly, later Advaita also formulates a formal proof on ground of such memory—*smaraṇaliṅgānumāna*.

Now, the feeling of 'not having known anything' on waking —when modalised cognitions of this or that prevail—can be attributed to an awareness of this very absence of all knowledge, the subject being supposed to have evidenced the said absence.[21] But such absence need not be taken in a *negative* sense; it should rather be conceived as the indefinite mass in which specific cognitions remain in a *potential* state This exactly is denoted by *ajñāna* (nescience), in which—as Advaita states—the organ of psychic activity (*antaḥkaraṇa*) finds, as it were, its primal potential state (*kāraṇāvasthā*). This vague awareness of undefined 'something', viewed in the light of modalised cognitions, assumes the more explicit form of 'knowing nothing' or 'not knowing anything'.[22]

That sleep cannot be regarded as a mere blank state has been shown from an analysis of the verdict of one awake from sleep. It can neither be urged that any judgment on sleep state can be passed on the basis of *stable* memory. The latter would hardly be possible, because the psychic organ, which alone can be the bearer of memory-giving traces, ceases to function in *suṣupti*.[23] Whether it can be regarded as *memory* in a loose sense or not, the supposed awareness of an indefinite mass is to be admitted as yielding some sort of cognition, wherein the mass should itself be regarded as content and apprehension in one. The later Advaitic explanation in terms of nescience-mode (*ajñāna-vṛtti*) also necessitates the positing of evidencing principle other than mind and ego. For, the element of *personal* consciousness or I-feeling is rather absent during deep sleep state—as may be testified immediately on waking, when a vague awareness of the surrounding objects prevails without any determinable I-feeling. Turning to the Yoga explanation, the mental mode of sleep, though having the notion of negation as content (*abhāvapratyālambanā vṛttiḥ nidrā*),[24] has still to be evidenced by *Puruṣa* (vide infra, *sākṣin*).

An analysis of the apparently negative experience of sleep significantly reveals the latter to be a stage of definite dissociation from the objective manifold. The content here is farthest removed from the object of waking perception, pointing to the possibility of consciousness being capable of remaining unmodified by the epistemic object. The compulsive and explicit character of the latter gradually subsides in steps of dream and sleep, without the corresponding evaporation of subjectivity.[25] Of course, a *conscious* withdrawal from objectivity, accompanying *definite* realisation of pure subjectivity, is not yet posited. Sleep state conveys the hint of untarnished subjectivity peeping faintly, as it were, behind the dark ground of *ajñāna*. But the background is yet to be *concretely* realised. All that is felt is the necessity towards a possible transcendental stage where subjectivity may be attained through conscious withdrawal from objectivity—the so-called fourth (*turiya*) stage.

In the characteristic classification of fourfold experience—originally given in Māṇḍūkya Upaniṣad—the phases of consciousness in different attitudes have been shown. The waking (*jāgrat*) state is characterised by the consciousness of external objects other than cogniser himself (*svātmavyatirikte viṣaye prajñā*). In the dream stage, marked by internally directed consciousness (*antaḥprajñā*), we are aware of mental states, more inward than sense-organs (*indriyāpekṣayā antaḥsthatva*). The sleep state, where the subject is not inclined towards the object nor does it see any dream, is marked by consciousness as unified (*prajñānaghana*). But with consciousness in a condensed state, self is as good as unmanifest at this stage *suṣuptāvyākṛtayostu ekatvam siddhameva nirviśeṣatvāt*).[26] To sum up from our discourse above, consciousness as unified in sleep, however bare it may be, is to be regarded as 'not a mere thought, an unreal abstraction, but a concrete reality', as K. C. Bhattacharya puts it (*Studies in Vedāntism*. Ch. I).

Now the element of bliss (*sukha*), said to be involved in sleep, should be considered in this context. Free from tension due to subject-object relationship, a state of mental rest may prevail in sleep. Still it should not be explained as a mere case of 'want of suffering (*duḥkhābhāva*). Similarly as nescience, positive bliss is also postulated on the basis of a feeling of 'absence of pain' on waking.[27] *Suṣupti*, so far as it provides a point of inwardization of consciousness, makes for *bliss*—though in a feeble way —which is conceived in the Vedāntic tradition as essentially centred in the nature of self. As *Vivaraṇa* remarks, seated in the innermost core of self, which as such is supremely 'desirable', bliss that otherwise remains hidden behind the turmoil of empirical experience makes itself felt during the unperturbed state of sleep.[28] However the fringe of happiness, provisional (*anātyantika*) as it is in deep sleep, carries only the hint of perfect bliss as the *ideal* state.

A NOTE TO CHAPTER I

The threefold approach to pure consciousness developed so far—particularly the last two—may be viewed largely with reference to relevant psychological evidences. Nevertheless, the approach should sharply be distinguished as such from what may strictly be regarded a *psychological* approach to the question. For the latter might as best show *cit* as a principle to be derived through relevant psychological analysis of mental states — chiefly by way of *introspection.** Thus for instance, a possible attempt to trace bare awareness 'without an object' by starting from a particular perception of object, could hardly be regarded as leading to the Vedāntic *cit.* For, even the alleged 'pure consciousness' so discovered would prove to be, after all, a *psychic state,* which cannot possibly be dissociated from the empirical (psycho-physical) context of the individual. However, such approach may yield a suggestion regarding 'consciousness without an object' as a psychological possibility—a point often missed in modern psychology.

---

*Cf. Girindrasekhar Bose, "Is Perception an illusion ?", *Indian Journal of Psychology,* July 1926, where a psychological approach through introspective experiment to the thesis of " pure consciousness" has been given. But such attempt to trace *bare* consciousness "without an object", by starting from a particular perception of object, can hardly be regarded as leading to the Vedāntic *cit.* For, pure consciousness supposed to be discovered on this introspective-psychological approach would, after all, prove to be a *psychic state,* which again cannot possibly be absolutely dissociated from the empirical context of the individual. Moreover, the intermediate associative, ascertaining and apperceptive levels in the region of consciousness cannot also be overlooked.

However, from the said approach we can gain a valuable suggestion as to "consciousness without an object" to be a psychological possibility—a point that seems to be so widely missed in modern psychology. This, of course, does not justify the contention : "Since the Brahman is of the nature of pure consciousness, any psychological experience when deeply introspected is likely to lead to the realization of the Brahman." (G. Bose, "The Psychological Outlook in Hindu Philosophy", *Indian Journal of Psychology,* July and Oct., 1930; Presidential Address, Sectn. of Psychology, Indian Philosophical Congress, 1930).

NOTES AND REFERENCES

1. "*.. jñātur arthaprakāśasya jñānatvāt tasya ca ātmāśrayatvāt, antaḥkaraṇapariṇāme jñānatvopacārāt*", *Vivaraṇa*, I, p. 41.
2. "*.. viṣayagatatvāt ākārabhedasya saṃvidaśca anākāratvāt*", Jñānaghana. *Tattvaśuddhi*, Ch. 33, p. 209.
3. Cr. "*Jñāte tu viṣaye paścāt anumānāt jñānam avagacchati*", *Śābara-Bhāṣya, Pūrva-Mīmāṃsā-Sūtra.*
4. Cf. *Śāstradīpikā*, I, i. 5 (*Tarkapāda*).
5. Sadānanda, *Vedāntasāra* (ed. M. Hiriyanna), p. 7f.
   N.B. Statements attributed to different sub-schools of Cārvākas need not be taken historically, but rather as 'logical stages in the progress of thought' in its approach to the true self, beginning with the primary belief in the selfhood of the body. cf. Hiriyanna, Notes to *Vedāntasāra.*
6. S. Alexander, "Self as Subject and as Person". *Proceedings of Aristotelian Society*, 1910-11.
7. *Cf.* "*.. bālasthavira-śarīrabhede api soham iti ekasyātmanaḥ pratisandhānāt dehādibhyo bhedena asti ātmānubhava*", *Bhāmatī, Adhyāsabhāṣya,* S.B.B.S p. 14.
8. S.B., *Kaṭh. Up.*, II. i.3. (*Śāṅkara-Bhāṣya-* referred to as S. B.)
9. S. Alexander, *ibid.*
10. G. Ryle, *The Concept of Mind*, ch. vi (6, 7).
11. "*Aśakyanirvacanīyebhyo dehendriyādibhyo ātmānam pratīpam nirvacanīyam añcati jānāti iti pratyaṅ sa cātmā iti pratyagātmā*", *Bhāmatī, Adhyāsabhāṣya.* (Here the stress is, of course, on the distinction of self from the empirical associations; but the definiteness as pertaining to the former is also in view).
12. *Bhāmatī, Adhyāsabhāṣya,* p. 30, p. 45. Also cf. *Pañcapādikā*, p. 17 (*idamanidamrūpa-vastugarbha*).
    Cf. "*Tena anyonyādhyāsāt cidacidgranthirūpaḥ adhyāsaḥ*", Madhusūdana Sarasvatī, *Siddhāntabindu* (*Tīkā* on *Daśaślokī*) *I.*
13. *Pañcapādikā* also refers to *ahaṅkāra-granthi*, p. 29.
14. "*Asmatpratyayatvābhimato ahaṅkāraḥ*", *Pañcapādika, p.* 17.
15. "*.. ahaṅkāragranthir asmatiśabdasamśabditaḥ pratyayaścāsau ādarśa iva pratibimbasya anidamcitsambalitatvena tasyābhivyaktihetutvāt*", *Pañcapādikā, a.* 29.
16. "*.. ātmacaitanyasaya savikalpatayā sphuṭīkaraṇavyavahāranimittam bhāsvaradravyam ātmanyadhyastam antaḥkaraṇam asmatpratyayam*", *Vivaraṇa* I.
17. *Ibid.*, p. 68.
18. W. James, *Psychology*, p. 157ff.
    N.B. From the strictly Behaviorist point of view, sleep and what Pavlov and his followers call 'internal inhibition' are one and the same process.
19. Śaṅkara remarks : In the dream state, the subject puts the body aside, as it were, and itself creates a dream-body of mental dispositions (*vāsanāmayam svapnadeham māyāmayamiva*) in its place, presiding over it as self-manifest. *S. B., Bṛhadāraṇyaka Upaniṣad,* IV. iii. 9.

20. S. B. B. S., III. ii.3.
21. Idem.
22. "*Avasthāviśeṣa-viśiṣṭasya ajñānasya suṣupte anubhavāt tasya ca jāgaraṇe 'pi ghaṭādijñāna-virodhitādarśanāt paṭāvagamasamaye*", *Vivaraṇa* I. p. 57.
23. In some later Advaita works, two types of Nescience—primal (*mūlājñāna*) and explicit (*tulājñāna*)— have been distinguished. 'Anything' in the expression 'not knowing anything' refers to, by way of implication, many objects not known; while such expression as 'I have been ignorant' refers to primal nescience as the content. Vide Madhusūdana, *Siddhāntabindu* (46-51), ed. A. Sastri (Calcutta).
24. *Yoga-Sūtra*, I. 10. N.B. Negation here should not be taken literally but rather to mean the element of *tamas*, which stands in the Sāṅkhya philosophy for the anoetic principle of obscuration. Cf. Vācaspati Miśra's *Tīkā* on *Yoga-Sūtra*, I. 10.
25. Cf. Śāṅkara's remarks that the self, though continuing through different stages, yet is itself beyond them as detached from all associations due to waking and dream experiences. ("*Sthānatrayavyatiriktatvam ekatvam śuddhatvam ca siddham*", S. B., *Gauḍapāda-Kārikā*, I. 1).
26. S. B., *Māṇḍ. Up.*, 3-4.
27. "*Anubhūtameva sukhamutthitasya anusmaryamāṇam tatra virodhiduḥkhābhāvam arthāpattyā gamayati anubhūtam cet sukham nāsti duḥkhamiti*", *Vivaraṇa* I. p. 56.
28. "*Bhāsata eva paramapremāspadatvalakṣaṇam sukham tīvravāyuvikṣiptapradīpaprabhāvat mithyājñānavikṣiptayā na spaṣṭam avabhāsate suṣuptau tu tadabhāvāt adhikam vyajyata*", idem.

Chapter II

PURE CONSCIOUSNESS IN THE PERSPECTIVE OF COGNITIVITY

In establishing the validity of consciousness (*cit*) as pure subjectivity in its autonomous essence — as attempted in the last chapter — one primary question remains to be answered. From the general line of approach we have adopted above — more explicitly through the analysis of knownness (Sec. A, Ch. I) — the essence of consciousness seems to be envisaged in *cognitive* terms. In other words, the supposed essence of consciousness is at the same time taken as equivalent to knowledge (*jñāna*). (The essentially self-evidencing character of *cit* as implied by its possible autonomy of status is shown in the next chapter through analysis of self-consciousness or reflective cognition, which also suggests a purely cognitive approach to the question.) What, then, is the justification of the formulation of the essence of consciousness in the light of cognition, i.e. *cit* as equivalent to *jñāna*, if the latter itself is regarded as one of the aspects of the totality of mental life ? This brings us to the question of ascertaining the position of *cit* in the total context of mental (or conscious) life. If consciousness essentially denotes subjectivity as autonomous, this status of consciousness has to be shown in relation to the totality of conscious life in its cognitive as well as non-cognitive phases.

So the question arises : is not knowledge just one aspect of mental activity, like feeling and willing ? Then, if *cit* is to be admitted as the generic background of mental states in general, why should it be equated to *knowledge* alone to the exclusion of the other aspects of the mental life ? Now, this claim of knowledge to be identified with consciousness entails an investigation into the true status of knowledge in relation to the non-cognitive aspects of consciousness. Accordingly such questions would have to be considered : Has knowing as a mode of consciousness a natural priority over feeling and willing ? If so, would such priority leave room also for a co-ordinate status among the three faculties of mind ? Lastly, the central question : Has knowledge any special character that it should be equated to *cit*-essence ?

So far as the general standpoint of western psychology is concerned, the three elements of cognition, emotion and volition are looked upon as mentally co-ordinate. There need not be any intrinsic or absolute priority of the one over the other. Consciousness in general, when admitted,—and admitted as an ultimate fact and as such logically indefinable,—is taken to be involved in or running uniformly through all the three kinds of mental states—cognitive, emotive and volitional. Each of the three aspects of mental life is equally an instance of consciousness — each an original co-ordinate form of consciousness.

Now, to concede priority to *knowing* over willing and feeling would amount to the admission that the two primary modes of mental activity other than knowing are reducible, on ultimate analysis, to *knowing* as the fundamental mode. And this is the position adopted in broad by different schools of Indian philosopohy—perhaps with the notable exception of Buddhism.*

Let us examine first whether the primacy of the mode of knowing can be held even at the empirical (psychological) level, without bringing in the standpoint of evidencing subjectivity. The issue may primarily be approached in the line of Nyāya-Vaiśeṣika, which is otherwise radically opposed to the Advaitic standpoint of *cit*. Though a transcendental status of consciousness as beyond the conscious states themselves is denied outright by the Naiyāyika, the knowing aspect of consciousness is still recognised to be virtually *primary* in relation to feeling and willing aspects. Some grounds for such contention may, of course, be shown.

---

*According to the general theory of *skandha* in the early phase of Buddhist philosophy, the four non-material factors (*skandha*) of existence, such as *vedanā* (feeling), *sañjñā* (perception), *vijñāna* (consciousness) and *saṃskāra* (mental concomitants), stand on the same level in the constitution of personality (*pudgala*). Any subjective state, it is held, is as much a self-subsistent phase of mental life as the other, being in no way considered as a condition of thatother—each suchstate subsists by itself[1].

(a) According to the Nyāya-Vaiśeṣika position, knowledge (*jñāna*) or cognition (*buddhi*) is a specific quality (*viśeṣaguṇa*) of self-substance and is consciousness itself-Self is not conscious (*cetana*) by itself; it is only regarded so inasmuch as it has the capacity (*yogyatā*) of possessing the quality of consciousness locatted in it. Moreover, such other mental qualities of self as pleasure, pain, desire etc. are also regarded as conscious, so far as they too are the specific qualities of the self that is conscious in the sense mentioned. It follows that though non-cognitive mental states are not by themselves conscious, the conscious character is attributed to them because of their common inherence (*sāmānādhikaraṇya*) in the self-substance along with the quality of consciousness. Knowledge thus proves to be more primary than the other mental qualities of self.

(b) Mental states of the volitional type—such as wish, aversion etc.—all presuppose the cognitive moment. Both Nyāya and Advaita agree in the contention that wish is due to cognition, because it is only when an object is previously *known* that we can wish for it and act accordingly. ("*Jñānajanyā bhavet icchā icchājanyā kṛtirbhavet*".) Even though in the case of feeling, a reference to object apparently belongs to such states as pleasure, pain etc., the reference actually pertains to the cognitive mode presupposed by such feeling.

(c) The distinction of level between knowledge of knowledge and consciousness of pleasure, pain etc. evidently comes out even from the analysis of the Naiyāyika himself. Thus, while the awareness of the inner states of mind is regarded as internal or mental perception (*mānasa pratyakṣa*) which is as much unreflective as any external perception, the knowledge of knowledge by way of retrospective evidence (*anuvyavasāya*) is unambiguously recognised to be a case of reflection. *Anuvyavasāya* is not just another name for internal perception. Knowledge admittedly presents the unique occasion for reflective consciousness. The question of *validity* (*prāmāṇya*) proper arises in the case of knowledge alone—validity which is sought to be proved by recourse to retrospective evidence. Internal evidencing and retrospective evidencing—the two apparently differ, one not having and the other having a necessary bearing on the question of validity. *Anuvyavasāya* could be at most regarded as a type of *mānasa pratyakṣa*. Even then it is to be admitted that while the awareness of pleasure, pain etc. may not amount to reflection, the awareness of knowledge cannot but be reflective. The former may as well remain uncertified, but the latter must necessarily be certified.

However, the knowing mode is not merely taken as prior to other modes of mental activity but also as co-ordinate with the latter. The common psychological contention is also not left out. To consider the Nyāya-Vaiśeṣika position first, knowledge is taken but as a specific quality of self along with other qualities. Besides the quality of cognition (*buddhi*), there are those of pleasure (*sukha*), pain (*duḥkha*), desire (*icchā*), aversion (*dveṣa*), will (*prayatana*) etc. Of these, *buddhi* stands for cognition, *sukha-duḥkha* for emotion and *icchā* and *yatna* for volition. (The position of *dveṣa* or aversion in this connection is rather ambiguous—it seem to stand midway between feeling and willing.) Cognition has the distinguishing character of manifesting or apprehending things, while the non-cognitive states show a different character.

Advaita would in broad agree with the Nyāya position, though through a different approach. A cognitive state is regarded as much a modification of the internal organ (*antaḥkaraṇa vṛtti*) as a state of feeling or of willing. The only difference between the two sets of modes—cognitive and non-cognitive—is that while cognitive modes (*vṛtti*) take on the forms of the corresponding objects outside, mental perception presents no object besides *vṛtti*.[2] But as *vṛtti*, both types of modes equally prove to be media for reflection of the evidencing consciousness. It is only as revealed by the latter that a *vṛtti* amounts to a state of consciousness in respect of modes of cognition and of non-cognitive modes as well.*

Here a question would arise : if a state of feeling or willing be alike a *conscious* state and as such involving in common the

---

*It has rightly been admitted by Advaita that mental states of pleasure, pain etc. are revealed to the subject as soon as they are generated. Internal states being generated in the psychic organ mean their being at once evidenced by the subject—no intervening factor of *ajñāna* being there to be removed, as in the case of cognition.

essential element of consciousness (whether *transcendentally* or as abstraction), then why are the former not regarded also as knowledge ? Is not the perceptual character of immediacy present also in feeling and willing ? Here comes into view the unique capacity of revealing the object—a capacity that characterizes knowledge alone as distinguished from feeling and willing. It is only through the act of cognition that object gets maifest to subject. The object that was previously unknown is presented to consciousness, or in the language of Advaita, the nescience (*ajñāna*) regarding object is removed through the relevant cognitive mode. But so far as emotive and volitional modes of consciousness are concerned, they hardly present this object-manifesting character through the removal of corresponding nescience.[3] (The said non-cognitive modes in the form of internal mental states have even been regarded by the later Advaitins as *avaidyā-vṛtti* rather than *antaḥkaraṇa-vṛtti.*)

So, through cognition alone is object manifested—and not through either feeling or willing. We *feel* necessarily an internal state of our own mind; even when in feeling there is a reference to object, it is but distant and indirect. In willing, however, an object is anticipated in imagination, but even that does not mean the actual presentation of the object. Empirically speaking, the manifestation of object through willing is hardly a possibility any more than through feeling.*

So, the fundamental character of empirical knowledge is the presentation of object; it is thus that the use concerning object is possible. And, in this respect, it has a marked semblance with the alleged evidencing by *cit.* It is in the essential character of manifestation (*prakāśa*) that consciousness stands equivalent to what we commonly regard as knowledge. However, the level of *cit* qua transcendental subjectivity, evidencing ultimately every mental state, and the epistemic level of the modalised psychic state, counteracting the

---

*The primal act of reference—*ikṣaṇa*—as spoken of the Supreme Self (cf. *Brahma-sūtra,* I. i.5) should not be taken too easily in the light of *empirical* willing. In the former, unlike in the latter, the primal act of creation is to be conceived as a *free reference* on the part of the Supreme Being—which may be considered as much an act of knowing as one of willing.

ignorance in respect of particular object, are to be kept apart. As one Advaita thinker remarks, the term *jñāna* is used in three different senses which are to be carefully distinguished.[4] The primary unreflective context of mere empirical use concerning the object present can hardly be treated as cognition proper—though *vṛtti* is nevertheless there. But such mode may be regarded as knowledge only in its apparent capacity of effecting the use of the object concerned.[5] However, the apprehension proper of *vṛtti* qua psychic state as we get it in introspection grasps *vṛtti* necessarily *as conscious*, i.e., as fused with the evidencing consciousness. But the mere *vṛtti* of the unreflective level, just effecting the directedness towards the object in use, seems to be *inferred* rather than directly apprehended as such.* Proceeding further, there is the transcendental level of pure evidencing by itself — *pratyak-bodha* — behind all particular modalisations in this or that form, external or internal. Here is *jñāna* in the higher sense of pure evidencing ground — *prakāśarūpatva*, and not in the epistemic sense of just removing the corresponding nescience—*ajñana-virodhitva*.

Now, it is chiefly in terms of *vṛtti* that cognition is brought on the same level as the other two types of mental activities. While in external cognition the psychic mode is distinguishable (at least *ideally*) from the corresponding object that occasions the mode, in internal experience of feeling and willing the two are not so distinguishable. Both the types, however, belong to the same status so far as the evidencing subjectivity is alike traceable behind both of them as their evidencing ground.

But the very principle of *vṛtti* as mediating between subjectivity and object may be held in doubt. The case of cognition, no doubt, brings out the question of *vṛtti* into relief. Is it necessary to admit *vṛtti* as the *tirtium quid* between the two poles of evidencing subjectivity and the evidenced object, as it is admitted in case of cognition ? The larger

*Sarvajñātma-muni make an evident distinction between *vṛtti* as such and *vṛtti* as psychic state. But the former is possible only on abstraction (vide our remarks on *vṛtti-cit* relation, *infra*). However, as a *formal* classification, the threefold division may stand.

issue of correlation of subjectivity and object here comes into view.

The realist like the Naiyāyika and G. E. Moore of modern times would oppose such mediating principle. According to them, the mediation of *vṛtti* is unnecessary for the experience of object. For consciousness, as taken to be 'diaphanous' in nature by Moore, is directly determined by the object present; there is no 'via media' between the object and the knowing mind. According to Moore, 'sense-data' are 'directly present' to mind. But it follows from Moore's point of view that knowledge-situation is just a simple direct relation (of course, external) between two objects—one physical and the other mental. Consequently, 'direct presence' suggests rather a spatial relation. But, neither can knowledge be regarded as a spatial situation, nor can the uniqueness of the factor of consciousness be overlooked. Moore's explanation of the situation seems to be rather too simple.[6]

To turn to Naiyāyikas, instead of admitting a mediating factor between consciousness and object, they would rather speak of the *'form'* (*ākāra*) of knowledge only as produced by the object concerned. According to the Nyāya theory, knowledge is just an originated entity (*janya-padārtha*) having for its occasioning factor some object outside, directly affecting the mind. But how far are we justified in regarding knowledge as an entity which is just caused ? (The point of view has already been met in Ch. I.) Whatever is there as effected through some cause must necessarily be varying according as the occasioning cause varies. From an objective point of view, knowledge may no doubt be explained in the light of varying objects. And the Naiyāyika account of knowledge in terms of the series of antecedent connections (*saṃyoga*)—beginning with the outer terminus of object (*artha*) and ending with self (*ātman*) *via* sense-organs (*indriya*) and mind (*manas*)—seems rather *external*, not having direct bearing upon the essence of knowing situation. That knowledge can possibly be viewed in its pure domain of subjectivity has been shown in the previous chapter. So viewed, knowledge reveals an intrinsic nature; and in the light of that nature the object-counterpart would prove to be just contingent.

However, the question remains: if knowledge is essentially homogeneous, how are we to account for the obvious distinctions in knowledge ? The realist like the Naiyāyika would be answering it in terms of difference in relation between knowledge and object, from instance to instance. And that difference is in the long run attributed directly to the difference of objects. But such Naiyāyika contention hardly stands scrutiny. Firstly, the Naiyāyika himself has to recognise *qualitative* difference in knowledge—perception (*pratyakṣa*), inference (*anumāna*), testimony (*śabda*), memory (*smṛti*) etc. being each a different kind of knowledge. It may be the same object that is referred to in perception, in inference and so on—the kind of knowledge varying even when the object remains the same.

Further may arise the question : even if it be admitted that the distinction between one knowledge and another is due to the difference of object, how is the relation itself (between knowledge and object) to be explained ? The said relation may not be recognised *qua* relation at the level of bare perceptual knowledge. Still it need not be denied that the relation could be so grasped at a further reflective level. Thus, in one case there would be the simple judgment 'there is X', while in another case the corresponding judgment shall be 'X is *known* by me'. The difference is not merely a verbal one, because the emphasis is shifted from the bare assertion of object in one case to that of the *knowledge* of object in another. This shows that knowledge stands not merely in the context of object but also admits of being grasped *subjectively qua* knowledge—as in self-conscious reflection (a point to be treated in the next Chapter). The Naiyāyika, like any realist, is wedded to the *empirical* aspect of knowledge—an aspect that only refers to the object and its use. Once, however, the subjective moment of knowledge is also recognised—as has in fact been recognised even by realists themselves, like the Naiyāyika (in the form of *anuvyavasāya*) and Alexander (in the form of 'enjoyment)'—the relation with object becomes a real problem. (See Chapter III).*

*Also cf. G. E. Moore, who recognizes "knowing" as distinct from the 'known', though he takes the relation between the two as "a simple and

The answer to this problem concerning knowledge-object relation may be sought for in a third factor, viz., *reference* of knowledge to object. (Even Moore recognises a third factor as subsisting between the consciousness and the corresponding object, mutually independent as the two are.) But *reference* itself as the third factor may again be understood either subjectively or objectively. Either *reference* may be taken to be a phase of the object itself, coming in relation to the knower. Or, it may be regarded as hinging on to knowledge and as such pertaining to the subjective side. From the former position it follows that reference belongs to object ; but the reference of knowledge would be hardly intelligible (a point examined earlier—Ch. I). Such reference may rather be viewed as pertaining to knowledge, while object as independently existing would practically turn to be *indefinite*. Thus, *vṛtti* as the mode of reference of subjectivity to object would prove to be the mediating factor as between subjectivity and object.*

So the status of *vṛtti* is to be understood as accounting for the apparent relation of subjectivity to object. (The phenomenological status of *vṛtti* vis-a-vis subjectivity is to be further clarified later—Ch. V.) *Vṛtti* enjoys the unique status of a mediator between the two poles of subjectivity and of object.[7] Viewed in its objective moment of reference, *vṛtti* appears for all practical purposes to be non-different from the object itself. Perhaps to make out this point in too vivid terms, it is held in *Vedānta-paribhāṣā* that in the process of perception the psychic organ (*antaḥkaraṇa*) is *projected* through sense-organ and

---

unique relation". Moore, however, goes too far in positing the existential independence of object and consciousness—merely from the fact that the awareness is of the object. (vide Duccasse, loc. cit.).

*The Sāṅkhya system also introduces—somewhat in the manner of Advaita—the third factor of *vṛtti* for relating the variable aspect of objects to the invariable aspect of *puruṣa* or subject as pure consciousness. *Vṛtti*, formed in the image of the object, is incorporated by *puruṣa* by way of reflection (*pratibimba*). But in Sāṅkhya theory *vṛtti* is not directed to the object outside; its *modus operandi*—from the level of *indriya* upto *buddhi* - seems rather to be confined within the domain of *subjective* experience. Thus, unlike in Advaita, the objective moment of reference seems to be overlooked--and therein lies the chief difference from the Advaita treatment of cognition by way of vṛtti.

assumes the form of the outer object. Cf. Ch. on '*Pratyakṣa*'.] But the subjective moment of reference is nonetheless there, with the result that *vṛtti* is sought to be grasped *qua* psychic state in distinguishment from object. At this phase—a phase of reflection—*vṛtti* appears to be fused with subjectivity, or in other words, what is present is *vṛtti-pratibimbita-caitanya*. This proximity of *vṛtti* with evidencing subjectivity—a proximity which is to be traced to the psychic organ itself—is also responsible for the evidencing of the object whose form *vṛtti* assumes.[8] *Vṛtti* is thus finally to be understood in the light of evidencing subjectivity itself. The fuller bearing of this *cit-vṛtti* relation can be brought out only when we consider the principle of nescience (*ajñāna*)—a problem which is left for a subsequent Chapter (Ch. V. 4).

Thus, in this chapter, further steps towards establishing *cit* as the principle of autonomous subjectivity are sought to be clarified. Firstly, an attempt to determine the exact position of *cit* in mental life has been made, and in doing so, to demonstrate the unique position of knowledge in relation to feeling and willing. Secondly, the role of *vṛtti* as the mediating principle correlating subjectivity and object is shown.

At this stage of our investigation we have to note that in all this attempt to model *cit* in the light of transcendental subjectivity, the *epistemological* question as such is not to be regarded as the first and foremost concern in Advaita Vedānta. It is, of course, true that the *cognitive* orientation, which can be regarded as the mainstay in the Advaitic doctrine of *Cit*, could by and large be translated in the usual epistemological language based, as it would be, on the subject-object dichotomy. Yet, as our study may eventually show, the transcendental status of consciousness (or pure subjectivity) cannot legitimately be read in such a manner as to exaggerate its *epistemic* role (a la Kantian model, more or less) to the exclusion of other possible dimensions. However philosophically important that role, it could still hardly overshadow the integral nature of *cit* in the constitution of the total reality of the human subject. The latter is not merely the knower; he is also — and in a significant sense — the affective and conative subject (see Ch. IV B). The consideration stated here would hold good in spite of recognising that Advaita Vedānta represents, as no other philosophy does, the exclusive thrust of knowledge (as *jñāna* is usually rendered) *par excellence*, that it is thoroughly a *jñāna*-oriented philosophy.

NOTES AND REFERENCES

1. Cf. "..*dhammā honti*", *Atthasālinī*, 155.
2. "*Sukhaduḥkhādi-avacchinnacaitanyasya tadvṛtti-avacchinna-caitanyasya ca .. aham sukhī ityādijñānasya pratyakṣatvam*" *Vedānta-paribhāṣā*, Ch. I (*Pratyakṣa*), p. 49.(ed. A. Sastri).
3. Vide Annotations by A. Sastri, *idem*.
4. Vide *Sarvajñātma-muni*, *Saṅkṣepa-śārīraka*, I, 179 :

   "*Buddhervṛttau jñānatā tāvadekā*
   Pratyagbodha jñānatā kācidanyā
   Tatsamparkāt jñānatā tatra cānyā
   Vyutpannoyam jñānaśabdastu tatra."
5. "..*vyavahāra-avisaṃvādād arthaprakāśātmatva* ..", *Rāmatīrtha-Ṭīkā, idem.*
6. Vide C. J. Ducasse, "Moore's The Refutation of Idealism", *The Philosophy of G. E. Moore*, ed. Schiipp, p. 242 ff.
7. "*Pariṇāmasya ubhayasaṃsargād* . . .", *Vivaraṇa*, I, p. 70
8. "*Antaḥkaraṇam hi svasminneva svasaṃsargiṇyapi caitanyābhivyaktiyogyatām āpādayati*", *idem.*

CHAPTER III

SELF-EVIDENCING *CIT VIS-A-VIS* SELF-CONSCIOUSNESS

As the essence of subjectivity, *cit* has been shown to have the possible *autonomy* of status, which would mean the certifying of *cit* by itself without the mediation of further epistemic process. It has already been observed earlier that *cit*-essence is involved in each conscious state generically—the invariable factor of *cit* and the varying modifications (*vṛtti*) of mental states forming a complex unity. Of the two factors, again, it is only to consciousness as the constant factor that the manifest aspect in psychic state can be attributed; and as such the former should not necessitate a further evidencing factor for its own manifestation, for that would be simply unwarranted. Consequently, consciousness which underlies (*anuvṛtta*) all psychic states as foundational subjectivity stands to be accepted as intrinsically self-evidencing (*svaprakāśa*).

The above thesis, put in broad argument, has to be substantiated by closely examining the larger issue in connection with the evidencing of consciousness. But the problem of *reflective* cognition may at once present an apparent challenge to such a position. That the primary unreflective experience is reflectively grasped by a secondary act of knowing seems to be a truism of the cognitive life. And such evidence of 'knowledge of knowledge' seems, on the face of it, to invalidate the thesis as to the autonomy and unobjectivity of consciousness. Firstly, to admit that a state of consciousness, to be evidenced, depends upon a secondary act of consciousness would mean surrendering the autonomy of consciousness in its supposed self-evidencingness. Secondly, the admitted amenability of consciousness to a secondary act of consciousness, i. e., its being a possible object of consciousness, might compromise its alleged unobjective character. Hence the question : is consciousness dependent on reflective evidencing, or as elf-evidencing is it not in need of an evidencing factor besides itself ? A precise answer to this question may go a long way to clarify the intrinsic *subjectivity* of consciousness.

The reflective level of consciousness, or what may be termed 'self-consciousness', may signify two situations : (a) knowledge or awareness of self. the subject; and (b) knowledge of knowledge, i. e., secondary knowledge concerning primary knowledge as the object. As we do not presume a metaphysical nature of self, the second part of the question alone, viz., the broad issue as to the knownness of subjectivity, assumes particular importance for our discourse. Self-consciousness is thus to be taken as the stage of reflective awareness, where the primary state of consciousness seems to be the object of a secondary instance of knowledge (whether by way of introspection or retrospection or some process of self-objectification). And such reflective level is, after all an undeniable fact so far as the verdict of empirical consciousness is concerned. Some significant explanations of the issue from standpoints other than that of pure subjectivity may here be considered before coming to the Advaitic approach to the question.

In this connexion, the view of Buddhist idealism (*Vijñānavāda*) regarding self-cognition comes into view. On the one hand, unlike the Naiyāyika realist, the Buddhist would recognise the intrinsic evidencing of idea (*vijñāna*); on the other, unlike the Advaitin, the Buddhist with his phenomenalistic attitude would never bring in the postulate of the constant evidencing background. The view of self-cognition (*svasaṃvedana*) is suggested as an alternative way—the view that consciousness as essentially atomistic knows itself in knowing its object. Every mental state has a peculiar self-grasping reflective character. However, the Buddhist idealist seems to share the Advaita view-point when he contends that the objects in view would remain unaccomplished in a knowledge which itself remains unevidenced.[1]

The inherent contradiction of knowing knowledge itself seems to be involved in the said view. Śaṅkara points out the contradiction involved in an act directed upon itself, the act and the agent concerned being identical—*svātmani kriyā-virodha*.[2]

In Buddhist mentalism, the necessity for the self-evidencing character of knowledge is indeed recognised but the *modus operandi* of such evidencing is conceived as within the context of mental states. Subjectivity is sought to be established on the level of psychic states—hence the apparent antinomy. The dilemma of introspective self-cognition would stand thus : either subject and object are identical, in which case cognition becomes an absurdity; or the two are distinct, which would not enable self-cognition at all.

The rationalist, in upholding the peculiarity of self-awareness, over-emphasizes the 'subjective' (i.e. mental) character of the introspected objects.* But to analyse such character, all that it may mean is the *privacy* belonging to the objects of introspection, being accessible only for the subject to whose experience-continuum they belong. However vague and undefinable it may seem to be, the characteristic intimacy of all intra-personal, as distinct from inter-personal, experience can hardly be denied. In every act of introspection there is present the characteristic flavour of selfhood. As on the one hand, the empiricist tries to explain the said factor away rather than explain it, the rationalist on the other would treat it on a *psychological* level, overlooking the epistemological *raison d'etre* behind it. In this respect, as we presently see, Kant's theory and more particularly, Advaita—with its conception of *sākṣin* as self -evidencing—can give a key to the peculiar intimacy as pertaining to the intra-subjective contents.

Again, a pseudo-idealist explanation on the matter may on the one hand recognise the subjective nature of consciousness and its capacity for effecting implicit reflection, and take such implicit activity of the subject on a level with the object cognised. Such a view-point is typically represented by S. Alexander and the Prābhākara school of Mīmāṃsā. The notion of "enjoyment", as introdueted by Alexander may be regarded as

*'Rationalism' has been used here in a broad sense which may include the Hegelian theory of self-consciousness (as mediated) and even in a sense, Gentile's theory of 'mind as pure act'—broadly those theories which in some way or other involve 'introspective monism'. All these views need not be discussed in the present context.

a further attempt towards explaining the phenomenon of self-consciousness. But, 'enjoyment' is, after all, hardly more than a feeling 'vitally' associated with the cognitive activity and as such cannot be taken as a mode of *cognition* on par with objective cognition or 'contemplation'. All genuine cognition is 'contemplative', according to Alexander. Moreover starting from the position that the mind is not to be regarded as a contemplated object to itself and that the acts of the mind are not to be placed on the same level as external things cognized, Alexander practically surrenders his position by allowing introspection too.[3] Besides, the term 'enjoyment' no doubt suggests a duality of the enjoying as the act and the enjoyed as the referent of the act.

In the Prābhākara theory of triple knowing (*tripuṭi-saṃvit*), we find a view on self-manifestness in line with Alexander's. The Prābhākaras advocate simultaneous revelation of the three factors in knowledge-situation—thing as object (*viṣaya*), knowing itself and self as the locus (*āśraya*) of knowledge. The manifestation of the knowing act is thus distinguished from that of either the object or the locus. Knowledge is self-manifest (*svaprakāśa*)[4], so far as its evidencing differs from that either of the object or of the locus.*

Now, the Prābhākara view, like Alexander's involves confusion of subjectivity and object in more than one way. Firstly, the manifesting activity of knowing, if it is to be at the same time a content of knowing—though not as external object—must surrender its essential nature as knowing. This is more evident from the fact that knowledge is practically regarded as on the same level with object. For the manifestation of knowledge as a separate factor goes necessarily with the manifestation of object. In the context of the latter alone does the evidencing manifest itself. Here a peculiar ambiguity in the Prābhākara position is to be noted. A purely *objective* attitude, like the Naiyāyika's (q.v. *infra*), may be intelligible—with its

*A distinction, however, is maintained between direct perceptibility (*saṃvedyatva*) and indirect knowability (*prameyatva*), whereby the primary act of cognition itself is made an object of inference.

unreserved emphasis on object, leaving knowledge primarily unevidenced. A thoroughly subjective attitude, as held in Advaita, would on the other hand lay complete emphasis on the *evidencing* aspect of the situation; and it is indeed from a more or less subjective attitude alone that the question of evidencing of knowing would assume importance.

The general doctrine of one-term self-cognition, in its various phases, thus involves subjective attitude in some form or other—with an appeal to introspection as admittedly the only epistemological approach to determine the nature of implicit reflection. There may, however, be a radically *objective attitude* in the explanation of the introspective situation, by taking it in the larger context born of knowledge-object relation. Accordingly the object apprehended is given emphasis and knowing as such turns to be a secondary question. Two broad consequences may follow in the shape of two possible views : (a) Introspection would lose any special position of its own, being a cognitive act similar to any objective cognition ; (b) Knowledge *as such*, besides manifesting the object in use, would prove epistemologically irrelevant.

In the first view mentioned above, a realistic analysis would show the conscious states of sensation, perception etc. to be directed to the respective objects but never to be self-cognizant. They may however be *reflectively* known through a subsequent retrospective act directed upon them. This is the realistic position of Nyāya in its theory of retrospective evidence (*anuvyavasāya*),* coming in direct conflict with the Advaitic position of self-evidencing subjectivity. According to Nyāya view, primary cognition is certified—if there is an occasion for so certifying—by a secondary cognition taking the former as its object. Thus, at the primary moment of awareness, we are just aware of the object presented, the cognition concerned remaining nevertheless uncertified. A secondary cognition is what is called for to evidence the primary one, and it is only at the

*It is more precise to render *anuvyavasāya* as retrospection, rather than as introspection, though epistemologically the two mean in essence the same situation.

secondary stage of retrospection that the primary cognition may be evident to us.

The Nyāya approach to the question bears evidently a realistic tone. Knowledge, for the Naiyāyika, can be as much objectified as an entity of objective experience. Knowledge is taken on the same level as *object*; and accordingly, the evidencing of knowledge stands logically on the same footing as the knowledge of external object. The only peculiarity of the former is that it is *reflective* apprehension of the latter. [Nyāya draws a clear-cut distinction between the reflective and the unreflective types of internal experience. Of the latter type is the internal perception (*mānasa pratyakṣa*) of mental states other than knowledge.]

The Nyāya view stated above is open to objection—particularly from a standpoint which is ready to take into consideration the unique character of the subjective pole of experience. Some of the salient points of criticism that Advaita puts forth against the Nyāya view may here be considered.*

A general criticism in the shape of a dilemma may at first be raised against the Nyāya view of retrospective evidence. Thus, to come to specific charges, if an instance of knowledge were admitted to be revealed by a knowledge other than itself, the latter again (i.e., the secondary cognition) — to be consistent — should be cognized by another instance of knowledge and that again by a fourth and so on. Thus would arise an infinite regress (*anavasthā*), leaving the primary knowledge which was sought to be certified, unestablished. On the other hand, if a subsequent certifying cognition be affirmed and yet the corresponding cognizance of the latter be denied, it would amount to an assertion of something, admitted knowable (*premeya-sattā*), without relevant knowledge of the same—a self-defeating contention to posit.[5] Even the realistic Nyāya-Vaiśeṣika system itself proceeds on enumerating the categories (*padārtha*) or knowables on the admitted principle of valid

---

*Cf. For a detailed account of the Advaita criticism against the Nyāya theory of *anuvyavasāya* and also for elucidation of the concept of *svaprakāśatva* author's article : "A Study on the Advaita Theory of knowledge: the concept of self-illumination", The Calcutta Review (April, 1954).

evidence in consciousness (cf. "*pramāṇebhyaḥ prameyasiddhiḥ*" etc).

From the strict common-sense point of view, however, the claim of *anuvyavasāya* seems to be unassailable, because knowledge is looked upon barely as a mental event, there being apparently no *a priori* necessity that this knowledge is to be evidenced. Yet the Naiyāyika candidly admits that there are also reflective judgments like "This jar is known" and seeks to explain them as evidently the result of retrospection. But it may be questioned whether what is predicated in the said judgment is *knowledge* as such or *object* known. An unsophisticated reply would, of course, be in favour of the latter. The realist, however, would further argue his point: knowledge can be understood on the analogy of sense-organ such as eye, which though acts as instrument for revealing the object to the knower itself remains unevidenced by the latter. But such an explanation would evidently bring knowledge to the status of instrument (*karaṇa*) of knowing, proving it to be an agent of manifestation rather than manifestation itself. This would indeed reduce the world as manifest to experience to be an absurdity (*Jagadāndhyaprasaṅga*). One Advaita author points out the possible infinite regress involved in taking knowledge to be merely the agent of manifestation (*prakāśaka*), not manifestation (*prakāśa*) as such. If knowledge be regarded as manifesting the object by way of producing another manifestation, the latter should similarly be taken to be producing another manifestation without being itself the manifestation. So it is to be admitted that knowledge being itself manifest can alone be regarded as evidencing the object.[6]

The other type of realistic view mentioned earlier is held by the Bhāṭṭa school of Mīmāṃsaka. It is more consistently objectivistic in outlook and close to the point of view just stated and criticized. The Bhāṭṭas take knowledge as necesarily beyond the grasp of direct awareness and only to be approached through the indirect way of inference. The Bhāṭṭas are well aware of the difficulties that follow the Naiyāyika view of retrospective evidence of knowledge; at the same time, the paradoxical position involved in the contention of Vijñānavāda is challenged. Thus the very possibility of evidencing knowledge is denied outright. The approach is rather from the side of *object*, to which the attribute of knownness (*jñatatā*) or manifestness (*prākaṭya*) is supposed to be added as a result of the knowing act.[7] It follows that the *unobjective* pure aspect of knowledge is not felt at all in cognitive experience.

Apart from the difficulties in admitting knownness as *objective* quality (which have been previously discussed—Sec. A., Ch. I) the cancellation of direct knowability of knowledge also can hardly stand examination. How can knowledge, itself remaining unevidenced, enable the use of object—and such use necessarily as known ? To agree to the Bhāṭṭa position would practically mean that knowledge is ever unmanifest. The difficulty of regarding knowledge as by itself unmanifest and yet manifesting the object would reappear. Moreover, the Bhāṭṭa attempt to establish the existence of knowledge by ignoring its subjective character and by looking upon it as a thing among things betrays their false approach to knowledge. For on their admission, though knowledge is as unmanifest as any object, it is yet not evident to us as the object is; and to that extent at least, knowledge would stand by implication on a different level. The difficulty with the Bhāṭṭa is that in their attempt to grasp knowledge *objectively*, they have naturally failed and have recourse to inference as the only approach left. Besides, as shown earlier (Sec. A, Ch. I), it would be logically impossible to establish knowledge if we proceed by way of knowing knownness.

Having examined some of the objectivistic theories, we may now turn to the *transcendental-subjective* point of view as one finds in Kant's philosophy. The recognition of the purely subjective character of the thinking ego in his first Critique is what distinguishes Kant's doctrine from the views so far considered. Since pure ego or knower is not introspectible, the only self which could possibly become an object of introspection is the empirical self. The problem of self-consciousness in Kant thus assumes two forms on two levels—empirical and transcendental. On the one hand, there is consciousness of self as object of perception; on the other, reflective thinking on the transcendental level takes self as the *subject* of thinking. The *true* self of Kant stands only as the bare formal unity of consciousness, to be grasped through thought rather than through 'intuition'.

Thus for Kant, the only possible way to apprehend subjectivity is to *think* self as subject—not to *know* it. For, functional subjectivity as meant by 'transcendental unity of apperception' is hardly a concrete reality. What is missed in introspection is sought to be accomplished through thought. Though 'the analytic unity of apperception is possible only under the presupposition of a certain 'synthetic unity', the latter as the faculty of apperception is the understanding itself; and as Kant points out, 'our understanding can only *think*':[8] It seems that subjectivity is, to all intents and purposes, identified with thinking function in the Kantian doctrine—thinking that is itself thinkable rather than self-evident. The implicit unity of self-consciousness indeed remains more or less a logical problem—"a problem rather than a true datum, a problem which can be solved by recourse to inner sense", as a contemporary writer remarks.[9] The question, however, remains: does not the primacy of knowing function as disinguished from the known content imply a certitude of its own ? In admitting the impossibility of the self being caught in a process of so-called self-consciousness, Kant no doubt stresses the unobjectivity of self. But with his interest primarily in the forms of objectivity as effected through 'categories' of pure thinking, Kant stops short of *essential* subjectivity. Kant's *transcendental* interest hardly goes beyond the modes of functioning to the essence whose function is considered.

It is exactly this supposed essence of subjectivity on which Advaita lays its hold. Like Kant, Advaita would recognize the necessary epistemological shortcoming of *empirical* self-consciousness and also would agree with Kant on the point of implicit self-consciousness, necessarily involved in a conscious state. Kant and Advita alike recognize the unity of self-consciousness at the *transcendental* (not empirical) level, presiding over the mental states—the former in the concept of 'transcendental apperception and the latter in that of *sākṣicaitanya*.* But in

*The Advaita concept of self as witnessing subject (*sākṣin*) comes up in the next chapter (Section B); the self-evidencing aspect of subjectivity alone is here under consideration.

Advaita, unlike in Kant, the enquiry is centered not upon the activity in terms of which objectivity is translated and interpreted but rather upon the essence behind the activity. While with Kant the transcendental moment of such activity is *thinkable* rather than intuitable, with Advaita thinkability would be only a secondary approach to transcendental self-consciousness. In the Advaitic account, as we shall presently see, the question of evidencing knowledge itself would be irrelevant at the level of transcendental self-consciousness, not because the latter is the 'logical precondition' but because it is essentially self-evidencing.

So, we come to the standpoint of *svaprakāśatva* as the typical Advaita answer to the question of evidencing of experience. Advaita would deny the possible approaches to the question other than its own, primarily by direct appeal to the element of *immediate certitude* involved in conscious act. The subject grasps the object through the act of cognition, but the act itself need not be grasped by another act of cognition.[10] Transcendental consciousness is to be conceived as the foundation behind the conscious life, beyond which there can be no further background—at least within the realm of personal experience. It cannot be taken as entailing another act of cognition; for that would mean either that a second cogniser is there to cognise the primary subject or that such cognitive act pertains to the self-same subject. But the former alternative would lead to an infinite regress of cognizer behind cognizer, and so on,[11] while the latter would[12] imply evident self-contradiction (*svātmani kriyā-virodha*) of cognitive acts—one taking the other as its object in the self-same agent of cognition. The difficulties involved in the realistic view of retrospective evidence and in the Buddhistic theory of self-cognition are duly noticed by the Advaita thinker. Accordingly, nothing short of foundational subjectivity involved within each state of consciousness is stressed, and to the former pertains the self-evidencing (*svaprakāśa*) character. Only as *transcendentally* involving the essence of consciousness, can a cognitive state—nay, any psychic state—claim to be self-evident.

Some initial doubts may, however, be raised against the concept of *svaprakāśatva*. Thus, with reference to the analogy of lamps in connexion with the concept, it may be urged that the apparent self-assurance and self-intimation of mental states would hardly justify the postulation of the 'phosphorescence character' of consciousness. But it may be replied that the analogy of lamp has in fact been excluded from the scope of *svaprakāśatva* as defined by Advaita. For, the characteristic of 'invariable manifestation'—the alleged contention of what Ryle would call the 'efflorescence theory' — would indeed prove to be too wide for defining consciousness as such, because mental states would also be covered thereby.[12] For, as noted in the last Chapter, mental states of feeling and willing generated in psychic organ (*antaḥkaraṇa*) are admitted to be necessarily evidenced by consciousness and as such remaining manifest.[13]

Some further charges may possibly be brought against the notion of *svaprakāśatva* from the realist point of view.* (a) A thing being illuminated and a mental process being conscious are not similar, because while illumination has degrees, there is nothing such for consciousness. The mental process being conscious presents itself immediately, while an object which is externally illuminated does not do so. On external analogy alone can the illuminated thing and the conscious state be considered as similar. As Ryle observes. "...Knowing is not the same sort of thing as looking at and what is known is not the same sort of thing as what is illuminated." (*The Concept of Mind*, p. 161). (b) Failure and mistake in the recognition of a mental state—a common fact of experience—seems to counter the contention of self-luminosity.

Now, as to the first charge, it seems to support rather than to rival the position that the evidencing of knowiedge is itself a peculiar self-assurance that brooks no mediation. Advaita indeed stresses that the self-evidencing character of knowledge stands unique in its immediacy and as such is not comparable to the illumination of things by light. The second difficulty, however, brings us to a larger problem as to the presence of *unreflective* mental states. It is a truism that there may be instances where we make use concerning a particular object without a 'recognizable' awareness of that object, while at some subse-

*The first objection stated here follows Ryle's criticism of the efflorescence theory' (*The Concept of mind*).

quent moment the original experience, not primarily noticed, becomes distinct. How is the presence of such *unreflective* level of experience, where awareness is seemingly absent, to be reconciled with the position that any instance of knowing is necessarily self-evidencing ? For, the use of object would entail the presence of the corresponding psychic state (*vṛtti*) ; and the latter once there could hardly remain unevidenced.

Here the peculiar *negative* bearing of the principle of nescience (*ajñāna*) on the evidencing consciousness is in view. Without going into an analysis and justification of the concept of *ajñāna* in Advaita philosophy, it may here be mentioned that it is meant to explain the apparent limitation of the pure evidencing character of consciousness as subjectivity.* As consciousness is the *raison d'etre* of the knowledge-of-object situation (shown earlier in Chapter I), the criterion for explaining the alleged irregularity in the evidencing of the object cognised should be sought for in consciousness rather than in the object. Thus from the Advaita point of view, the explanation would be in terms of some lapse, as it were, of the evidencing consciousness through an *alogical* factor, i.e., *añjāna*. Consequently, the object would appear obscure, though from the side of object there could be nothing to prevent it from being revealed to cognizer.[14] So experience, when it does not appear to be quite explicit, would be inexplicable except through the recognition of 'functional negativity' involved within experience. And the subsequent awareness of the previous unreflective moment should rather be understood as a case of *retrospection* of the earlier mental event. It is not reflective in the sense that the primary awareness is made an object of secondary awareness.

Now, after meeting these relevant doubts, we come to the notion of *svaprakāśatva*. It has been defined (in "*Citsukhi*") as 'the capacity of immediate use without being cognizable' (*avedyatve sati aparokṣavyavahārayogyatvam*).** Formal as the

---

*For the status of *ajñāna* in relation to *cit*, vide Ch. V.

**This standard definition, accepted in later Advaita, is so formulated by Citsukhācārya in "*Tattvapradīpikā*" after considering other possible, but inadequate, attempts at defining the notion of *svaprakāśatva*. (Vide *Citsukhī*, pp. 3-21).

definition is, it seems to characterize consciousness rather in a negative manner by way of differentiation (*vyāvṛtti*). Chiefly concerned with avoiding the defects as in other views on the evidencing of consciousness, the definition seems to miss the *positive* essence of consciousness. 'Uncognizability' and 'the capacity for immediate use' should be taken as the *external* characterization of knowledge that may prove helpful in excluding it from the *empirical* notions. As already remarked, the character of *svaprakāśatva* should be confined to foundational subjectivity behind psychic states appearing to be conscious. To the level of mental states (*vṛtti*), which serve as the media for reflecting consciousness, may however pertain manifold grades of cognition varying from the unreflective to the explicitly reflective. It is thus evident that pure consciousness as self-evidencing marks a level distinct from that of modalized mental states.

Where is then the point of departure for the transcendental self-evidencing level ? Here the negative epithet of 'uncognizability' can certainly provide a clue towards understanding the positive import of *svaprakāśatva*. It signifies a departure from the common objective attitude of grasping things; for, naturalistic attitude is apt to miss the essence of knowledge. The possibility of *indirect* cognition through intellectual comprehension need not, however, be denied; what is denied here is *direct* cognition. In indirect cognition the object in context is apprehended through *vṛtti*-mediation and not directly revealed to consciousness—it is *vṛtti-vyāpya* and not *phala-vyāpya*, to use the later Vedāntic terminology. But the common notion of objectivity includes not only thinkability but also the possibility of being perceived as object. (Cf. Kant's distinction between thinking and knowing : "To think an object and to cognise an object are by no means the same thing". However, with Kant, knowledge is only with regard to the object of possible experience, i.e., sensible intuition.) Here on the other hand, perceptuality is completely denied and thinkability alone retained. Pure consciousness cannot be revealed by pure consciousness itself. One may still refer to pure consciousness as capable of immediate use only so far as *immediate certitude* pertains to consciousness and thereby renders it amenable to cognitive judgment.

From the Advaitic account of self-consciousness given so far would follow the approach through *pure psychology* as distinct from empirical psychology. On considering the subjective functions of knowing in referential relation to various modes of *knownness* (or types of *objectivity*), we may pass on to the level of subjective activity as such—in dissociation from the objective givenness. Here comes into view what may be characterized as 'transcendental psychology' or 'spiritual psychology', as termed by K. C. Bhattacharyya (Cf. *The Subject as Freedom*, p. 27ff). Its distinction from ordinary empirical psychology is sharply brought out in its being founded on the thoroughly subjective attitude. The subjective functions of knowing, feeling or willing are commonly understood in psychological and epistemological considerations as associated with *objects* known, felt or willed. But here we find an attitude which sharply turns from object and aims at the pure essence of subjectivity. Consequently would come into play the approach through gradual unobjectification along with inwardization.

Some of the Upaniṣads, and Śaṅkara in his commentaries, emphatically urge the deepening insight with a view to obtaining higher and higher levels of spiritual truth. In pointing out the significance of the scriptural texts, differentiating the true self from other physical and psychical adjuncts, Śaṅkara remarks that they (scriptural texts) intend to direct the mind towards the innermost self (*pratyagātmābhimukhikaraṇārtha*).[15] Knowable categories—from the level of senses up to the level of intellect (*buddhi*)—are regarded as so many approximations to the core of subjectivity. Accordingly pure self (*ātman*) should stand at the upper terminating point in the series. And each higher level in the hierarchy is ascribed excellence in relation to the lower, till the innermost self is attained as the highest of all excellences in the individual.[16] The enumeration of the steps in the hierarchy is meant to prompt the mind which is naturally in the outgoing attitude, to turn towards self.*

The essential self has indeed been declared as the innermost self (*pratyatgātman*). Self is denoted as innermost (*pratyak*),

---

*Further (phenomenological) significance of the steps in the scheme of Advaitic metaphysic of experience shown later (Chs. V and VI).

making itself immediately felt to be certain as distinct from the complex of psycho-physical associations which is not so immediately felt—("*Aśakyānirvacanīyebhyaḥ* etc."—see Ch. I. B). The character of self as differentiated from the outer is explained as being due to the association of consciousness with ego, the latter necessarily positing itself in differentiation from the objective world outside.[17] Senses are naturally directed outwards and as such hinder the approach to self within. It is not possible for one, intent on external objects, to be at the same time approaching the inner self. And hence the instruction to the aspirant after self-realization for suspension of the naturalistic attitude (*svabhāva-pravṛtti-nirodha*).[18] In strengthening further the motive for such attitude, Śaṅkara of course refers to the alleged target of immortality (*amṛtatvam*), cited in the Upaniṣad, meaning the constant character pertaining to the core of individual existence (*amaraṇadharmatvam nityasvabhāvatvam*).[19] Thus the approach to the true self marks a positive departure from the objective attitude. And that is what is implied by the Advaitic doctrine of *Cit* as *self-evidencing*.

NOTES AND REFERENCES

1. Cf. "*Apratyakṣopalambhasya nārthadṛṣṭiḥ prasidhyati*", Dharmakīrti, *Pramāṇvārttika*.
2. S.B.B.S., II. ii. 28.
3. S. Alexander. *Space, Time and Deity*, vol. I, Introduction.
4. "*Mitau ca kācidanupapattir nāsti iti svayaṃprakāśaiva mitiḥ*", *Śālikanātha*, *Prakaraṇapañcikā*, ch. IV (1).
5. "*Anubhūteranubhāvyatve anavasthāpātāt na ca vācyam, avaśyavedyatvābhāvāt na anavasthāvyavahārasya tatsvarūpasattāmātreṇāpi upapattiriti. Tadviṣayapramāṇānudaye tatsattayā api aniścayāt tata eva vyavahāra ityapi asiddheḥ*", *Citsukhī*, I, p. 15.
6. "*Tataḥ pratibhāsamānasyaiva jñānasya tatsādhakatvam vaktavyam*", Jñānaghana, *Tattvaśuddhi*, ch. 35, p. 19.
7. Citsukhācārya, the Advaita thinker, has represented *jñātatā* as self-manifest (*svaprakāśa*), vide *Citsukhī*, p. 18. (But that would not be in strict conformity with the Bhāṭṭa view).
8. Kant, *Critique of Pure Reason*, "Transcendental Deduction", trans. N. K. Smith, p. 153 f. (Macmillan, 1953).
9. W. H. Walsh, *Reason and Experience*, Ch. IX.
10. Vide S.B.B.S., II. ii. 28, and *Bhāmatī* thereon.
11. *Bhāmatī*, loc. cit. : "*na ca pramātari kūṭasthacaitanye pramāpekṣasambhavaḥ, yataḥ pramātuḥ pramāyāḥ pramātrantarāpekṣāyām anavasthā bhavet*".

12. Vide *Citsukhī, I*, p. 4: *sukhādau ativyāptiḥ sukhāderapi svasattāyām prakāśa-vyabhicārāt*".
13. *Ibid.*, p. 4f.; also, cf. author's article, "A Study on the Advaita theory of knowledge : the concept of self-illumination", *The Calcutta Review*, April, 1954.
14. Cf. "*Anātmapramāṇasya caitanyasya vaikalyādāvaraṇādeva viṣayānavagatisiddhiḥ na viṣaye pṛthagāvaraṇam kalpanīyam*", *Vivaraṇa*, I. p. 14.
15. S.B.B.S., I. 1. 31.
16. *Kaṭhopaniṣad, I.* iii. 10; also, S.B. on the same.
17. "*Ātmanastu sarvātmakatvāt na parāgvyāvṛttatā, ahamuparāgādeva vyāvṛttyava-bhāsaḥ*", *Vivaraṇa*, I. p. 55.
18. Cf. "*Parāñcitkhāni vyatṛṇat svayambhūḥ tasmāt parān paśyati nāntarātman. Kaściddhīraḥ pratyagātmānam aikṣat āvṛttacakṣuḥ amṛtatvamicchan*", *Kaṭhopaniṣad*, II. 1. 1. & S. B. thereon,
19. *Idem.*

Chapter IV

SELF IN THE LIGHT OF PURE SUBJECTIVITY

Our enquiry so far shows consciousness, in its ultimate essence, to be nothing but self-subsistent and self- evidencing subjectivity. But consciousness, after all, is primarily to be understood in the context of *self* as the locus—a point previously noted (Ch. I). No doubt, only as pertaining to self, the subject of experience, could consciousness signify subjectivity. Now as consciousness itself proves on ultimate analysis to be unobjective, the conception of self too would necessitate modification in that light.

In positing metaphysically the epistemic principle of *subject*, we come upon *self* as embodying substantive identity. The question remains as to how to relate such self with consciousness in the light of subjectivity. In this regard a kind of dilemma seems *prima facie* to follow: Self is commonly supposed to be the locus of consciousness; if the essence of pure consciousness be approached in completely *subjective* terms, how could its locus be defined in *objective* terms — which would mean subjectivity abiding objectively? On the other hand, to be merely the locus of consciousness would mean distinction, rather than identity, of the two—self and consciousness; and if consciousness proves to be ultimately nothing but subjectivity *itself*, self should not similarly be looked upon as subjectivity—two 'subjectivities' as such being an apparent absurdity.

So it seems, the way to resolve this problem lies in a revision of the common notion of self in relation to consciousness. Moreover, a possible metaphysic of experience, seeking in consciousness the essence of subjectivity, may ill afford the notion of self as a mere 'metaphysical' principle, not innerly connected to an analysis of experience. So the definition of self in the light of a critique of experience is necessitated. Accordingly, the *phenomenological* correlation of the two principles of self and of consciousness has to be shown (Sec. A) and then the resulting orientation of the import of self would follow from such correlation (Sec. B).

SECTION A. EQUIVALENCE OF SELF AND CONSCIOUSNESS

Self in its common import means the substrate of consciousness rather than consciousness itself—the latter being regarded as quality, either essential or inessential. To deny consciousness in self altogether would, on the other hand, go contrary to the apparent fact that the *experience* of things, as distinguished from things themselves, does occur in the 'person', commonly accepted as self. Thus, short of unqualified identity of self and consciousness—which is exactly the position of Advaita Vedānta,—we are left with the alternative of viewing consciousness either as essential or as adventitious attribute of self. Above the phenomenalistic extreme would appear the intermediate group of views—realistic and semi-idealistic—represented by Nyāya-Vaiśeṣika, Prābhākara Mimāṃsā, Rāmānuja etc. All of them would agree more or less that self is a substantive entity, but refuse to identily it with consciousness*. Self is *metaphysically* posited to be the locus of consciousness taken as attributive—either accidentally or essentially. How far this difference of self and consciousness may be allowed is to be considered here—particularly in the light of the Advaita criticism on the point.

According to Nyāya, consciousness belongs to self as accidental attribute—self in its essential nature being nonconscious (*jaḍa*). Consciousness is regarded as extrinsic quality (*āgantukadharma*) originating in the soul-substance. It is looked upon more as a phenomenon occurring to soul-substance rather than a self-accomplished (*parinṣṭhita*) principle. Knowledge is but the resultant of a series of relations (*saṃyoga*), of which self is the last term just preceding mind-organ (*manas*). As for the persitent identity

*For Rāmānuja, unlike Nyāya etc., though self is taken to be necessarily conscious and even 'self-manifest' in that sense (Cf. "*Cidrūpatā hi svayamprakāśatā*"), consciousness is conceived essentially aș *attributive* (*viśesaṇa-bhūta*) and self, its locus, as the knower implied by 'I' (Cf. .. na *jñaptimātra-mātmā apitu jñātaivāhamarthaḥ*").

of self, implied by the phenomenon of *memory*, it may be accounted for by self being a permanent substance (*nityadravya*) which remains constant behind mental states. Moreover, the intrinsically unconscious (*svataḥ acetana*) nature of self is sought to be proved by an appeal to the instances of sleep, swoon etc., during which self, it its contended, evidently lacks in consciousness.* Thus self being sometimes found conscious and sometimes not, the Nyāya realist prefers to take the conscious character pertaining to it as extrinsic and adventitious (*kādācitka-caitanyatvāt āgantuka-caitanya ātma*).[1]

Now to the Nyāya position stated above, the question would arise as to how self, being devoid of the conscious character, is in a position to recognize the past experience as its own and connect it with the present state of consciousness. The Nyāya-Vaiśeṣika realist seems to prefer the path of commonsense in accepting the apparent phases of conscious and non-conscious states and in postulating—rather in abstraction—self as the *neutral* repository of such (passing) phases. But the point remains that we hardly posit self except as intrinsically conscious. For the 'dark' inert substratum — even if metaphysically posited—would be (epistemologically) unintelligible from the point of view of evidencing. Moreover, the explanation of consciousness through the mechanism of *saṃyoga* seems to be rather mechanical and to underestinate the *sui generis* nature of consciousness. To pass from the antecedent process which can be explained in purely *objective* terms to the sphere of consciousness which can properly be understood only as subjective would hardly be an intelligible transition. Moreover, as regards the status of consciousness itself, its reduction to mere 'epi-phenomenon' could hardly be admitted even by the Naiyāyika himself. For, it would be hard to reconcile such position with the Naiyāyika contention that consciousness is the condition for positing the objects of experience (*q.v.* Introduction). To derive consciousness completely in terms of objective factors, which

---

*Bhāṭṭa Mīmāṃsakas also prove the non-self-evidencing nature of self from the fact of non-experience of self during sleep—"*suṣuptau aprakāśāt na ātmanaḥ svaprakāśatvam*", *Śāstra-dīpikā*, (Nirnayasāgar), p. 100.

themselves presuppose (at least epistemically) consciousness, seems to be an obvious contradiction.

As regards the state of deep sleep or of swoon, the apparently felt absence of consciousness therein may be interpreted as the lack of *object* rather than of consciousness. When the object to be evidenced is not there, the evidencing principle as such does not seem to be quite evident.[2] The Naiyāyika seems to confuse the lack of the referent of consciousness with the absence of consciousness itself. Again, so far as the reference-character pertains to knowledge, it belongs *mutadis mutandis* to self, the admitted locus. Thus self comes to refer to object by way of knowledge-relation.* A knowledge-situation may simply be viewed in the light of a lamp illuminating a thing, say a jar. Further, in a given knowledge-situation, the object as known may be taken to be manifest by the subject concerned —as implied by such judgment in use as "The jar is known by *me*". In this case a dichotomy between self and consciousness—self being divested of consciousness—would mean the manifestation of object by a non-manifesting factor. Then, why not admit a log of wood as manifesting the jar in context ? An unsophisticated analysis of the situation thus shows self to be the manifesting factor in a simple knowledge-situation, proving a schism between self and consciousness as unwarranted.[3]

Advaita further argues that if self were not intrinsically conscious, it would be liable to doubt and to contrary judgment. But there is no such dubitability with regard to the subject of consciousness, *i.e.*, self.[4] On the contrary, the positive character of immediacy and certitude as pertaining to self would come into view. Whether in inferring or in remembering or in doubting or contradicting with regard to this or that object, the knower himself remains all the same immediate, indubitable and uncontradicted.[5] And that is because self is of the very nature of consciousness itself, which is characterized by immediate certitude. Were self

---

*The point has been formally presented by way of *anumāna* against the Naiyāyika : "*Ghaṭa-tajjñānayoḥ sambandhaḥ ātmaniṣṭhaḥ jñānaniṣṭhatvāt padaviṣayatvavat*" (*Citsukhī-Tattvapradīpikā*, I, p. 22).

intrinsically inert and only accidentally conscious through acquiring an adventitious quality, doubt, mediacy, contradiction etc. should have necessarily followed.[6] Instead of doubt as regards 'I', the unmediated assurance regarding self presents itself to the individual in and through conscious acts. The experiencing agent need not be evidenced *separately* by an act of cognition, because it is the very evidencing itself.[7] [Free from doubt or contradiction, self is indeed denoted by the epithet 'self-evidencing' (*svaprakāśa*).]

To posit a locus for consciousness, however, seems to be quite a common tendency in philosophical as well as in common-sense thinking. Thus for the Prābhākaras, consciousness, though regarded epistemologically unobjective, is yet taken to be abiding in self. While knowledge is admitted to be revealed unobjectively in immediacy, self though recognised to be immediate without being object of knowledge is still taken to be revealed as the *locus* and not as object. But the Prābhākara distinction between locus and object appears to be only half-drawn. That the supposed locus of consciousness could come under the broader category of objectivity is not duly considered by the Prābhākara thinker. To be an *object* in the widest possible extent would hardly exclude the locus from its scope.

Moreover, so far as self proves to be immediate only in the context of the knowledge of *object*, the intrinsic immediacy of self as *subject* is evidently overlooked. Again, on the Prābhākara admission itself, immediacy without being object of consciousness—a character admittedly pertaining to the latter—would belong to self as well. This as such precludes the necessity of drawing any distinction between consciousness and self, if the Prābhākara is to be consistent.[8]

The manifesting character (*prakāśaguṇatva*) of consciousness is admitted in common by Nyāya and Prābhākara as by Advaita; but the uniqueness of this character is overlooked by the former. Even in the empirical context, such character should be distinguished from any other empirical quality; and its distinguishing mark would lie in perfect coincidence with its supposed locus in respect of origination or appearance. Thus, as in the case of a lamp (whose very nature is luminosity), in self there could be origination of the manifesting quality only with the origination of self.[9] But so far as self is admitted to be eternal, *i.e.*, without an origin,* it follows that the manifesting quality cannot be regarded as having a separate origin of its own; hence consciousness, the said manifesting character, should be regarded as identical with self.

As to the *apparent* origin and destruction of knowledge, such temporal determinations are to be understood only in the light of modalized consciousness represented by the modifications of psychic organ and not to be referred to consciousness as such (as pointed out in Ch. II). The two levels of consciousness—empirical and transcendental—here come into play. Consciousness as empirically detetmined would correspond to objects and may be spoken of as appearing and disappearing—its intrinsic essence being left apart. But so far as consciousness in its self-evidencing essence is concerned, it would admit of no empirical, temporal determinations.[10] The varying, contingent, temporally determined character of consciousness comes rather from the *objective attitude*, while in its unobjective essence consciousness is to be posited as immutable — (" ... *viṣayagatatvāt ākārabhedasya, saṁvidaśca anākāratvāt*").[11] In the latter aspect alone is consciousness equated to self, whereas in the former it *apparently* is located in self in its varying phases.

In positing that self is manifest in the cognitive act as the locus along with the object, the Prābhākara really means the cognizer (*pramātā*) or ego (*ahaṅkāra*). That ego is manifest along with the object in cognition would be admitted by Advaita too.[12] But so far as the epistemological character of unobjective immediacy (*anidantā*) is concerned, Advaita would hold it as only *seemingly* pertaining to ego and not being the essential nature thereof. The Prābhākara, on the other hand, would practically go beyond the ego—the latter being left as the locus of knowledge. That this ego cannot

*The *eternity* of self, if it is to be non-metaphysically understood apart from any reference to scriptural authority, should be understood in the light of the essential undeniability of unobjective consciousness (*vide* Ch. I)

be identified with self, though naturally confused therewith, has already been shown in course of our discourse (Ch. I. B.).

Thus, an appreciation of the unique import of subjectivity should lead to the identification of consciousness and self. A difference between the two may be entertained only on a more or less objectivistic approach. But viewed from the standpoint of pure subjectivity, the seeming difference between knowledge and knower would pertain only to the superficial level where the subjective essence is missed. On an approach admittedly subjective, the epistemic dualism of knowledge and knower—though such dualism may not be so pronounced as that of knowledge and object—is sought to be reduced to the essential background of subjectivity; whereas in approaches that are not so, such dualism tends to stand (in most cases to be metaphysically justified in the long run).

Section B. The Concept of Sākṣin

The bridge between consciousness and self, the supposed locus, has been shown above—not externally, but in terms of the essential identity between the two on the level of pure subjectivity. Now *cit* as the ultimate essence of subjectivity tends to go beyond all reference to individuality, and so would self as non-different from such transcendental essence. As previously observed, all the empirical features that we associate with the individual—even up to the stage of mind—tend to be superseded in the pure essence of *cit*. The question, then, would arise : Should even the last vestige of individuality be possibly left out, as one crosses the threshold of empiricality to enter, so to say, the transcendental region of *cit* ? At this point comes in the cardinal concept of *sākṣin* or 'witnessing self'.

As Bṛhadāraṇyaka Upaniṣad (IV. iii) poses the question as to what the 'central light' may be, through which the individual comes to be evident (*kiṃjyotirayampuruṣaḥ*), the enquiry is set on foot after a principle, which though involved in the empirical individual, would yet stand beyond the confines of the latter.* Such 'light' is thus sought after, which may

*Śaṅkara, in his commentary, explains the light in question as that by means of which the individual carries all his actions (*vyavaharati*), S. B., Bṛ. Up., IV, iii. 2.

be more foundational than the light from external agencies—apparently enabling our perception of the external world. The said 'light' should be treated as different from the physical (*abhautika*), being unfailing in character (*aluptaśakti-svarūpatvam*) unlike physical agencies of manifestation. Self is pointed out as the evidencing agent in question (*ātmaivāsya jyotir bhavati*), departing at the same time from the *empirical* individual comprising the congeries of bodily and mental factors. Here self stands as the very essence of the individual which marks the link between the empirical and the metaphysical regions. Thus, on the one hand, *sākṣin* which participates in the process of empirical activity (*vyavahārāṅgatva*), cognitive or otherwise, is not taken as *completely* transcendent in character. On the other hand, *sākṣin* need not exhaust itself within the confines of the empirical individual (*jīva*). In approaching the concept of *sākṣin*, its *jīva*-transcending character comes first into consideration.[13] The primary point of departure in the question of *sākṣin* is the empirical individual, who not only cognizes but also feels and enjoys.[14]

The common import of the term 'witness' (literal meaning of '*sākṣi*) conveys the central characteristic implied by the notion of *sākṣin*, viz., seeing or experiencing without being agent of the act concerned (*akartṛtve sati draṣṭṛtvam*).[15]* Even as evidencing, it is a unique activity—an activity that implies no agency (*kartṛtva*). From the common-sense point of view, however, the cognizer would necessarily be involved in the act of cognition so far as the former is an agent of the act. The cognizer, for all practical purpose, shares the same level as the other epistemic categories, viz., cognition itself (*pramā*), the way of cognition (*pramāṇa*) and the object of cognition (*prameya*)—all veering round the cognitive act.** Now the transcendence of knowership in particular invites opposition from the realist

*Sāṅkhya also points to the *sākṣi* character of self (*puruṣa*) in a similar way "...draṣṭṛtvam akartṛbhāvaśca", *Sāṅkhya-kārikā*, 19.

**Vātsyāyana in the *Nyāya-Bhāṣya* expounds the four-fold categories enumerated here : and the scheme is *prima facie* accepted by the Advaitin too. Jñānaghana evidently has in view the four-fold categories when he refers to *sākṣin* as differentiated from cogniser etc. (*pramātrādi*).

camp. Thus, for the Naiyāyika, cogniser (*pramātā*) itself is experiencer (*draṣṭā*); even the subject of false cognition is no other than the cognizer itself, because the object altogether outside the scope of cognition can neither be the object of false cognition. Consequently, *sākṣin* as a distinct principle other than cognizer would be unwarranted.

The Advaita approach in reply would chiefly be with reference to the question of the evidencing of mental states, cognitive and otherwise. The plain acceptance of mind as the organ of internal experience (*antarindriya*) may explain—as in Nyāya—the internal perception of mental states through the medium of mind (*manojanya-pratyakṣa*). But such mental perception of non-cognitive states is sharply distinguished in Nyāya from *reflective* knowing or *anuvyavasāya*. Behind both these cases, however, what must stand in common is internal evidencing in some form or other. As for mental states like pleasure etc., they can hardly remain in the mind unnoticed. Even with their *seemingly* unreflective character, the emotive-volitional states of mind have sharply to be distinguished from unreflective sense-perception.

So, if both these types of apprehension—unreflective mental perception and reflective knowing—are characterized in common by *internal evidencing*, the law of parsimony (*lāghava*) demands that there should be postulated an evidencing principle more foundational than mental states (cognitive or otherwise) themselves. Such a principle in the background may be characterized in terms of 'knowing by way of immediate evidencing (*sākṣātkāri-jñānatva*). Of course, the possibility of evidencing, independent of mind, may well be questioned. It may then be replied that at least the state of deep sleep (*suṣupti*) (as discussed previously) presents an outstanding case, when nescience (*ajñāna*) itself seems to be evidenced as object—and when organs of valid knowledge (*pramāṇa*), nay the psychic organ itself, do not function.

The said evidencing principle may prove to be the transcendental precondition in all particular instances of perceiving. Three interpretations have been presented in later Advaita regarding the relation of self to object in perception, mediated through *antaḥkaraṇa*.* The peculiar association of *antaḥkaraṇa* with pure consciousness being granted, views may differ as to the exact process how *antaḥkaraṇa* serves to bring about the manifestation of object to subject. Nevertheless, the *transcendental* status and importance of *sākṣin* in perception is recognized in common; it is admitted to be the evidencing subject involved in each state and revealing the object by imparting immediacy to it. Common-sense philosophy tends (as noted in the last section) either to posit self in complete exclusion from the psychic process or to equate it altogether with the latter. But we need not proceed with any prior metaphysical bias towards soul-substance as *completely* detached from all psychic activities. For, the transcendental character of self as the ultimate pre-condition of subjective life should possibly emerge out of a reflective analysis of the conscious process involved in mental states.

To seek a near illustration of the point in concrete terms, anger or intense desire may be occupying my mind for a while, when I completely identify myself, without being aware of so identifying, with the passing mental phase. But as anger or desire cools down, I find myself in a position to reflect on the very outgoing state of mind as such. In so reflecting, I may by and by recognise the outgoing state as *my own*; and therewith in a glimpse, as it were, may be recognized the evidencing of the same state. Thus a notion of my 'inner consciousness' would come upon me—one involved in my mental states and yet found to be referring *freely* to such states.**

---

*Cf. Three sub-theories in Advaita as to the function of *antaḥkaraṇa* in perception and the consequent place of the individual (*Jīva*) in relation to the object in perception : (i) *abhedābhivyakti.* (ii) *ciduparāga* and (iii) *āvaraṇābhibhava.* Vide D. M. Datta, *Six Ways of Knowing*, Ch. IV ("The Place and Function of the Self in Perception").

**Perhaps the modern English poet drives at the same point as he declares:

> "To advance from friend to the composite Self
> Central 'I' is surrounded by 'I eating',
> 'I loving', 'I angry', 'I excreting',
> And the 'great I' planted in him
> Has nothing to do with all these." (Stephen Spender)

To trace the evidencing background of the experiences of self in and through psychic states, which stand necessarily evidenced, would be a continuous process of gaining essence, within the region of subjectivity. It is not a discontinuous leap in the dark for a self that lies in primeval inertness. The transition from mind to self has indeed been rather mechanically conceived in Nyāya-Vaiśeṣika. As directly stated in Yoga philosophy, the fact that psychic states appear necessarily evidenced points to the truth that the subject which 'owns' these states should be of a constantly evidencing nature ("*Sadājñātāḥ cittavṛttayaḥ tatprabhoḥ puruṣasya apariṇāmitvāt*", *Pātañjala-sūtra*, IV, 18).*

Against the Naiyāyika contention as to the possibility of mental perception (*mānasa pratyakṣa*) of self as qualified by mental states, Advaita argues negatively. The position that self as endowed with the attributes of pleasure, pain, knowledge etc. is knowable by the same self through mental perception, would involve the fallacy of contradiction of subject and object (*karma-kartṛ-virodha*). The same self is the *subject* of knowledge in question and, as endowed with mental attributes, is also the *object* of that knowledge. Again, to treat self under two aspects—pure and qualified—in order to avoid such contradiction, would be too sophisticated an approach.[16] Further, the *reductio ad absurdum* entailed by the Nyāya position may be put in another way. Knowledge, as the factor constituting the principle of cogniser (*pramātā*), admittedly shares the same level with other mental states like pleasure, pain, wish etc. Now, to regard such cognizer as cognizing the mental states themselves—may be through an organ other than sense-organ—seems apparently to involve absurdity.

Still, a reply may be found on the Naiyāyika side by referring to (after Ryle) 'higher order acts'. According to Ryle, who is certainly more radically positivistic than the Naiyāyika in explaining mental phenomena, "for any operation of any

*The contrary argument goes: had *puruṣa*, or the self as consciousness, been non-constant and contingent like other things, mental states would have remained at least sometimes unknown. (Cf. *Vyāsa-Bhāṣya* and Vācaspati, *Tattvavaiśāradī, loc. cit*).

order, there can be operation of a higher order". But such explanation would leave us with a series of cognitive acts without a unitary reference to an experiencing subject which may connect the series of cognitions (*anusandhāna*).* (Even Ryle, while explaining the phenomenon of self-consciousness wholly in empirical-psychological terms, refers to a 'witness'.)

Again, a reflective analysis of body-consciousness also (as already mentioned in Ch. I. B.) would bring home the unique unmediated evidencingness of the transcendental evidencer or witness. Individual cognitions in respect of the body may vary from one mode to another—each taking separately the body or certain of its aspects as specific object. Nevertheless, behind all specific modalities of bodily cognizance there remains implicit a generic awareness of the body. This background of generic awareness of the body, against which explicit cognition through specific modes occurs, is enabled through the unfailing unmediated evidencing by the constant (*kūṭastha*) evidencer.[17] During the lapse period between one specific mode of bodily cognizance and the next, the body remains all the same evidenced although implicitly. Thus, while consciousness appears in modes as varying and temporarily determined, it is found constant and invariable in its aspect of transcendental evidencing.[18]

Thus, behind the physico-mental complex commonly called the individual (*jīva*), there is to be traced the invariable background of consciousness subsisting essentially in unmediated evidencing.[19] This alone may be regarded as the inner essence of the individual which, as Śaṅkara points out (*Adhyāsa-bhāṣya*), evidences the series of mental states (*aśeṣa-svapracāra-sākṣi*). The inner self *owns* the states, but, itself being outside the stream, remains completely unmodified by the process. Consequently, the epithets 'detached', 'unaffected' etc., conveying the unique position of self.[20] At the same time, the constantly

*Cf. Apperceptive unity in Kant's "Transcendental Deduction"—the transcendental-functional substitute for substantive self. Kant's 'Unity of transcendental apperception' is in a sense, largely equivalent to *sākṣin* of Advaita—the question of metaphysical status being left apart.

evidencing character of the inner self makes itself felt with immediate certitude, ever indubitable and uncancelled.[21]

This unique relation of free and detached reference to the mental apparatus (*antaḥkaraṇa*) that acts only as the limiting condition and not as the qualifying attribute, has been brought out in a more formal manner by the author of *Vedānta-paribhāṣā* in his differentiation of *jīva* and *sākṣin* in relation to *antaḥkaraṇa.* Though *jīva* and *sākṣin* are not two different entities, both being grounded in consciousness (*caitanya*), they still indicate two distinct perspectives in which the foundational consciousness operates in mental life. While in the case of *jīva,* pure consciousness in all appearance is circumscribed by mind—*antaḥkaraṇāvacchinnam*—as the qualifying attribute, in the case of *sākṣin,* mind can at best serve as just the limiting condition—*antaḥkaraṇa-upahitacaitanya.* Thus while the qualifying attribute (*viseṣaṇa*) differentiates its subject as directly related to the function predicated of it—*kāryānvayi vartamānam vyāvartakam,* the limiting condition (*upādhi*) differentiates but is not connected with the function (apparently) predicated of it—*kāryānanvayi vartamānam vyāvartakam.*[22] This can be regarded as an appropriate formal-syntactical translation of the phenomenological situation pertaining to *jīva* and *jīva-sākṣin.**

At this stage, a further crucial question as to the possibly metaphysical status of *sākṣin* cannot possibly be evaded. Indeed for Advaita, *sākṣin* as the substratum of *individual* experience or being, need not be the last word. It may move even further to the *ideal* level of pure consciousness in its absolute autonomy, in which the evidencing act would not play a *constitutive* role. Following in this line, some Advaita thinkers draw a distinction between the dual aspects of *sākṣin*—transcendent and immutable (*kūṭastha*) on the one hand, and immanent and functional

*Extending this model of division to the cosmic (metaphysical) level in the total perspective of *Māyā, Paribhāṣā* similarly works out the distinction between God (*Īśvara*) as qualified by his power of creation—*māyāvacchinnam caitanyam,* and God conceived as the detached witness of his creative power—*māyopahitam caitanyam.* In other words, it is an analogue (and a projection) of what prevails on the *jīva* level—pure Consciousness remaining the foundational stratum in both the contexts.

(*taṭastha*) on the other.[23] According to this distinction, in the latter aspect alone does the notion imply evidencing function—and correspondingly, the evidenced continuum (*dṛśya*). In its ultimate nature as pure consciousness, however, self would involve no reference, even detached.

To sum up, so far as the essence of individual or 'person' is concerned, we could hardly stop short of pure consciousness. The latter constitutes the innermost being in the individual, though uniquely associated through free evidencing reference with the empirical manifold of bodily-mental factors—the latter being the apparent index of personality. The freedom of the evidencing act no doubt conveys the suggestion that self *per se* could *possibly* remain in transcendent autonomy—a state in which even the reference-act would prove to be irrelevant. Such *possibility* has already been envisaged in respect of consciousness. However, to pass on at once from *sākṣin*, the freely subsisting pure self, to the *metaphysical* principle of all-transcending Being, i.e., *Brahman*, would be too wide a transition to be justified in the present context.* Here, however, the essential nature of consciousness as subjectivity—a concept which may as such prove to be abstract—is sought to be defined with reference to the relatively concrete concept of *self*.

From our discourse in Part I, it finally comes out that the ultimate *essence* (the term 'essence' being used roughly, not strictly, in a *phenomenological* sense) of individuality would prove to be but pure unobjective consciousness (*cit*) itself. Viewed in the attitude of *object*, 'person' may be understood in terms of combined unity (not identity) of several factors, physical and

---

*However, Jñānaghana—and Advaita thinkers would generally agree in this respect—has defined the status of *sākṣin* in a two-fold way—epistemological and metaphysical, the former pertaining to *jīva* and the latter to *Brahman*. In anticipation of the metaphysical, the two aspects are thus sought to be reconciled. ("*Paramārthato brahmatyepi pratibhāsataḥ sākṣiṇaḥ samsāri-antarbhāva eva*", Jñānaghana, *Tattvaśuddhi*, Ch. 35).

mental. But viewed *subject-wise*—i.e., in the attitude which tends sharply to turn from object (as independently existent)—an analysis in search of the true essence of person should ultimately lead to pure subjectivity. *Cit* is thus sought to be posited as the *non-empirical* ground of the individual, who is otherwise necessarily connected with the world of empirical experience.

That there is possibility for pure consciousness, which is equivalent to the essence of subjectivity, to subsist in complete autonomy, has been sought to be derived through several independent approaches by way of analysing salient epistemological and psychological features and situations (see 3 sections, Ch. I). What is shown thereby is that consciousness, besides barely implying what is subjective, bears within itself the possibility of autonomously subsisting in its pure essence—completely unalloyed by any objective association whatsoever. Still the doubt may remain whether, and how far, the supposed autonomy of pure consciousness could satisfy the larger claim of being the essence of *all* possible phases of consciousness, unless it be clearly demonstrated not only with reference to cognitive phenomena but to mental states *in general*.

So, to avoid a possible confusion in understanding *cit* as the background of the total texture of mental life, its foundational position is shown in respect of all the three types of mental states (Ch. II). The autonomous status of *cit* as foundational subjectivity is further sought to be strengthened by an analysis of the phenomenon of reflective knowledge or self-consciousness (Ch. III)—the unique self-evidencingness of *cit* is brought out thereby.

Further, the alleged essence of subjectivity has to be set in the *concrete* context of the individual, who not only knows but also acts and enjoys. Hence the step towards further defining the principle of subjectivity in the light of self, the supposed principle of unity within the complex of physico-mental elements that roughly constitute *person* as individual. (Ch. IV).

NOTES AND REFERENCES

1. Vide Śaṅkara's statemcat of the Nyāya-Vaiśeṣika position, S. B. B. S., II. iii. 18.

2. Cf. "*Viṣayabhāvāt iyam acetayamānatā na caitanyābhāvāditi. Yathā viyadāśrayasya prakāśasya prakāśyābhāvāt anabhivyakter na svarūpābhāvāt tadvat* ..", S.B.B.S., II. iii. 18.

3. Cf, "*Pradīpena prakāśitam itivat mayā avagatamiti vyavahāradarśanāt. Ātmacaitanyayorbhede vyavahāro... upacāritaḥ syāt*", *Vivaraṇaprameya-saṅgraha*, p. 57f.

4. *Citsukhī*, I, p. 32.

5. Cf. "*Pramātā sandihānopi asandigdho viparyasyannapi aviparitaḥ, parokṣam artham utprekṣamānopi aparokṣaḥ, smaran api anubhavīkaḥ prāṇabhṛtmātrasya*", *Bhāmatī*, II. ii. 28.

6. Cf. "*Yadāgantuka jñānam jaḍasvabhāvam tat kadācit parokṣam kadācit sandigdham kadācit viparyastam, na caivam ātmā*", *ibid*., II. iii. 18.

7. *Cf.* "... *na tu upalabdhāram prati tatpratyakṣatvāya upalambhāntaram prārthanīyam*", *ibid*, I. ii. 28.

8. Cf. Vidyāraṇya's refutation of the Prābhākara view: "*Ātmā na saṃvidāśrayatvena aparokśaḥ saṃvitkarmatāmantareṇa aparokṣatvāt saṃvedanavat*", *Vivaraṇa-prameya-saṅgraha*, p. 85. Also, cf. Citsukha's formal argument against the Prābhākara on the point : "*Ātmā saṃvidrūpaḥ saṃvitkarmatām antareṇa aparokṣatvāt saṃvedanavat iti prābhākaram saṃvitkarmatām antareṇa aparokśatvāt saṃvedanavat iti prābhākaram prati anumānāt*", *Citsukhī*, p. 28.

9. "...*dravyajanmavyatireke svadravyopādhau janmābhāvasya pradīpādau dṛṣṭatvāt atrāpi jyotiḥśabdāt ātmani prakāśaguṇasya janmābhāvaniścayāt*", *Vivaraṇa*, I. p. 41. Also, cf. *Vivaraṇa-prameya-saṅgraha* : "*Pradīpagatabhāsvararūpavad.... ātmā eva anubhavaḥ syāt*".

10. Cf. "*Svayamprakāśasya janmavināśānupapatteḥ*", Jñānaghana, *Tattvaśuddhi*, Ch. 33, p. 208f.

11. *Ibid*, p. 209.

12. Cf, "*Jīvākārāhamvṛtti-pariṇata-antaḥkaraṇena ca jīvobhivyajyate*" *Vivaraṇa, I* p. 73.

13. Cf, "... *sākṣi jīvavyatirekeṇa vyavahṛyate*", Appayadikṣita, *Siddhāntaleśasaṅgraha*, I.

14. Jñānaghana poses the enquiry on *Sākṣin* with the question : "*Kim-pramātrādivyatiriktaḥ sākṣi nāma kaścit asti na vā*", *Tattvaśuddhi*, ch. 35, p.217.

15. Nṛsiṃhāśrama, *Advaitadīpikā*, I. p. 439.

16. Vide *Citsukhī*, IV, P. 38*lf.* : "...*mānasapratyakṣavedyatve icchādeḥ karmakartṛbhāvasya bādhakatvāt*".

17. Cf. *Pañcadaśī*. VIII. 1: "*Kūṭastha-bhāsito deho dhīstha jīvena bhāsyate.*"

18. *Ibid*, IV. 24.

19. Cf. "*Tam pracāram aśeṣam asaṅgitayā avikāritvena ca hānopādānaśūnyaḥ sākṣāt avyavadhānam avabhāsayati citidhātuḥ*", *Pañcapādikā*, p. 35.

20. Cf. "*Asaṅgitayā avikāraitvena ityādinā sākṣiśabdārtham āha*", *Vivaraṇa*; also "*sākṣāt īkṣaṇāt nirvikāratvāt* ca", *Siddhāntaleśa*, I.

21. *Bhāmatī*, II. ii. 28: '*Asya sākṣiṇaḥ sadā asandigdha-aviparītasya nityasākṣātkāratā anāgantukaprakāśatve ghaṭate*".

22. *Vedāntaparibhāṣā* of Dharmarāja Advarīndra—Chapter on "*Pratyakṣa*".

23. Vide *Advaitadīpikā* : "...*draṣṭṛtvaghaṭitam sākṣitvam na svarūpam apitu udāsīnabodhātmakameva sākṣitvam svarūpam, tasya niṣpratiyogikasvarūpatvāt*", p. 441.

PART II

VEDĀNTIC PHENOMENOLOGY

CHAPTER V

ADVAITA METAPHYSIC OF EXPERIENCE : PHENOMENOLOGICAL PROLEGOMENA*

I

TOWARDS ADVAITA PHENOMENOLOGY

What follows from our investigations in the preceding Part is not *cit* that should stand as a logical abstraction; nor does *cit* prove to be a metaphysical principle proper. For the interest has been focussed on *cit* as *the* essence of subjectivity rather than as the metaphysical *prius*. And so far as the possible status of subjectivity can *prima facie* assure a philosophical standpoint, the latter should enable a complete interpretation of the basic structure of experience. Advaita might therefore be regarded as adopting the standpoint of subjectivity proper when the chief features and knots pertaining to knowledge and experience could be shown to be resolved in the light of that standpoint. Thus a more or less self-complete system of criticism of experience in the light of a possible methodology (with its distinctive outlook on subjectivity and object) would come into view. There is no need of introducing any metaphysical postulations in the pathway of such a procedure.

---

*In our discourse in this chapter and the following' conceptual as well as terminological use of certain ideas and expressions, which are characteristic of the phenomenology of Edmund Husserl, has been occasionally made by way of free interpretation (and not strictly in the Husserlian or phenomenological perspective). The introduction of the phenomenological concepts in the Vedântic context has thus to be viewed only as a methodological aid in the in-depth understanding of the *cit*-centric philosophy of Advaita in its own terms—and not as a parallel translation, in juxtaposition, of the Vedântic doctrine as projected and reconstructed here.

Now, in order that the Advaita metaphysic of experience as a whole could be reorganized, the methodology that might be implicit therein has to be developed. Thus in the analysis of the structure of knowledge and experience a methodological direction in the unfolding of the foundationally operating notion of subjectivity could be traced out (as the epistemological-psychological analyses set forth in the previous chapters already indicate). Differing from common empirical psychology and epistemology, where the prior reality-status of actual object is fundamentally presupposed, such methodology (which is at the same time subjectively oriented), could possibly alone be in a position to retrace the subjective standpoint of Advaita as represented by the principle of *Cit*, and thereby to bring out the implications behind the epistemological-metaphysical tenets in Advaita philosophy.

Such a possible methodology, however oriented to subjectivity has still to be distinguished from a mere *psychological* analysis of mental states. A *transcendental* analysis of experience—be it Husserlian or Advaitic—should not be read in the light of psychological analysis but is rather to be taken as a system of truths whose validity, logical or ontic, would not be grounded in mental states and functions.

Now the philosophical discipline of Phenomenology could lend us such a broad methodological line of interpretation as needed for the purpose (See Introduction). A metaphysic of experience, if closely followed, should show in its development an *implicit* phenomenology (at least in a broad sense) and be understood in that light. Thus, once assured of the standpoint of subjectivity as involved in the Advaita doctrine of pure consciousness (*cit*), we should be in a position to attempt towards reorganizing the whole of Advaitic criticism of experience on the basis of phenomenological approach in the sense mentioned. However, no external comparison between Phenomenology and Advaita is in view here. The former could only throw light on the *implicit* methodology, along which a thoroughgoing metaphysic of experience within the framework of Advaita philosophy could be developed.

Indeed the phenomenological aim is to bring in no metaphysical postulates and to attain a possible system of absolute truths on a rigorous analysis of experience. And the aim of Śaṅkara also has been likewise to discover, as S. Radhakrishnan points out, '*the* immanent principle within experience' rather than to construct a world beyond it.[1] No postulate regarding the reality of *transcendent* object came in the way of Śaṅkara's analysis of the pure realm of inner experience

However, such an approach need not be understood as being motivated by an artificial attitude of suspense towards object—an attitude admittedly not natural. Any exclusive preoccupation with *theoretic* consciousness—as in Kant or in Husserl—would possibly entail some attitude of indifference, or suspension of belief, towards the naively accepted objective reality. Further, in Husserl the 'bracketing' of external reality is taken rather as a *theoretic* attitude to facilitate the mind in turning back within itself and inspecting it from within, as it were. In Vedānta, however, the attitude of turning from the flux of objective appearance is recognised to be a serious phase in the spiritual life of man and not merely a *theoretic* attitude. Śaṅkara lays down the avowed aim of his enquiry thus : to avoid the snare of the objective world, into which the self is dragged from its native home of pure subjectivity, and to restore subjectivity to its foundational source.[2] With Advaita, unlike with Husserl's Phenomenology subjectivity is not a mere theoretical presupposition, nor is the movement towards grasping its essence a purely theoretical attitude. One has to remember that, after all, Vedānta is motivated by the deeper interest in liberation (*mokṣa*), recognized to be the supreme value (*Parama-puruṣārtha*).

As indicated in the beginning of our investigations (see Introduction—p. 6), a twofold approach could be demonstrated as implicit in the Vedāntic scheme of a metaphysic of experience, in combining metaphysical transcendence to phenomenological immanence. Thus in its equation of *Brahman* (or *Ātman*) with *Cit* (or *cidātman*), the entire enquiry is already brought to the experiential level of individual consciousness, thus providing it the context of perceptibility (*pratyakṣatva*)—or in other words, *evidence*. So, instead of proceeding from 'above', it would now turn to be a movement from the 'bottom'—that is, from the level of givenness by way of being 'conscious of'. This latter phase (of ascent, so to say) could be described as broadly 'phenomenological' in the sense that in its enquiry into the central essence of subjectivity, proceeding from the continuum of empirical subjectivity, the methodological frame of reference is essentially provided by *evidence* in consciousness. In other words, the world of objects, of things and events, is not sought to be *explained* in terms of metaphysical theory, but rather—*described* qua phenomena given to consciousness, which at the same time meaningfully refers to them. It thus proves to be a movement from the *transcendent* to the *transcendental*, via the immanental of individual experience. (How far the said 'transcendental' stands rejoined to the original 'transcendent' is a question to which we address ourselves in the next Part of the book.)

2

The Method : Transcendental reflexion

As noted above, the realization of self, which in essence is pure subjectivity, is the avowed aim of Advaitic thought. And the pathway to such realization lies along inwardized reflexion. As shown in a previous chapter (Ch. III), Advaita insists on the mind's turning inwards towards grasping the true self. Such inwardization, however could proceed only at the cost of the natural objective attitude. But what would be the point from which the natural attitude turns to the transcendental ? For Advaita, the phonomena of error in our knowledge and experience would present such a turning point.

The phenomenon of error (*adhyāsa*) presents in the fact of contradiction a concrete occasion for *reflection**. As soon as the content of one experience is contradicted by another—the

*This would indeed justify Śaṅkara in introducing his metaphysical discourse with the problem of error. But the *Adhyāsa-bhāṣya* is more often than not taken rather too easily as just providing the key to the metaphysical solution of Advaita as to the appearance of world phenomenon (*jagat-prapañca*).

common locus of reference being presupposed—the subject is faced with a situation which demands reflection with a view to understanding. Thus the content of false perception comes to be recognized *qua* its false character, in contrast to the reality of the substratum. But the content of false perception *prima facie* comes to us as objective presentation and thus causes the 'shock' for common-sense in violently contradicting the stable objective character of things, with which we are familiar. Consequently, the need for reflection by way of turning back upon experience-content as such.

As with illusory appearance such as rope-snake, so with the confusion of bodily characters with the subject-self, the fact of contradiction would demand a suspense of the existential character of the presented content and a closer inspection of the content *qua* content. In case of body-self identity (*dehātmādhyāsa*), the native sense of subjectivity, although it does not prove by itself to be an objective presentation as such, would still clash directly with the objective character of body, senses etc. This a parent incongruity of the two moments within the given experiential situation seems to call for a closer inspection, and thereby a distinguishment of the constitutive essence from the constituted objective complex.

This line of approach through reflection may be more expressly formulated in terms of what may be characterized as 'transcendental reflection' (after Kant). A steady insight into the presuppositional ground or structure of possible experience as may be brought through close scrutiny of the contents within the region of consciousness—and not any mystical intuition of revelation—is what is generally meant by *transcendental reflection*. It is to be sharply distinguished, as Kant suggests, from *logical* reflection; for, the latter seeks to proceed by way of comparison of the given representations without taking into account the corresponding faculty of knowledge to which the representations belong.*

---

*By "transcendental reflection" in a subjectively oriented analysis of experience, Kant meant the principle of *distinguishment*, through which the given representations may be traced back to their respective faculties.

The threefold Vedāntic discipline in the steps of hearing (*śravaṇa*), intellection (*manana*) and contemplation (*nididhyāsana*) can be understood in the light of the said transcendental reflection. The chief stress in the tradition of Vedāntic discipline is on the cultivation of that attitude of mind—at varying levels—in which the pure and essential structures of experience could become evident. Of these, *śravaṇa* signifies in the long run the terminating point of enlightenment (as the Vivaraṇa school in particular maintains); the stages of *manana* and *nididhyāsana* serve as but instrumental means (*sahakāri*) thereof.[3] *Śravaṇa*, on ultimate analysis, would mean the reduction of intellectual truths to direct apprehension; but primarily it stands for the strictly *intellectual* level of acquaintance with relevant scriptural texts in their logical connexions. Intellection (*manana*) is supposed to reveal further the essential features behind the apparent truths of the scriptures; and through intense concentration (*nididhyāsana*), the whole mind is to be fixed on the essence or essences so discovered and get in tune therewith (*ekatānatvam*).[4]

Advaita keeps to the point that real enlightenment can come only through concrete intuition (*anubhūti*) and not through abstraction. As Śaṅkara urges, all empirical and logical reasoning must be reduced to intuition; because through that alone we are presented with reality.[5] Knowledge is to culminate in *complete* comprehension of the essence in view—"*Avagatiparyantam jñānam*" (S.B.B.S.I.i.l.). And this is the case not merely with the knowledge of *Brahman* but at every step of transcendental reflection along which Advaita approaches the highest essence. The true function of mental reflection passes from purely logical reasoning to the apprehension of essences in distinguishment from the associational correlates. *Pañcadaśi* (I. 37) clearly refers to this approach when pointing to the

Husserl uses the term 'reflection' or 'self-reflection' somewhat in the Kantian sense, meaning that type of conscious acts in which the stream of experience, with all its inherent phases, can be grasped and analysed in the light of its own evidence. Husserl describes it as "consciousness' own method for the knowledge of consciousness generally" (*Ideas*: *General Introduction to Pure Phenomenology*, p. 219 subsequently referred to as *Ideas*).

distinguishment of the essence of self in progressive dissociation from the associated strata (*koṣa*).*

Intuition for Advaita would not mean *a priori* intuition—either of the Cartesian or of the post-Kantian type, i.e., a higher type of intellectual activity or thinking elevated to the level of immediacy. Nor does it presumptively stand for any form of mysticism as such, in the sense of some supra-rational access to supernatural divine reality, and so on. All that would simply mean a surrender of the philosophic enterprise itself. The mode of Advaitic reflection, on the other hand, can philosophically be understood as a progression in the essence-wise comprehension of the immanently constitutive principle embedded in the region of pure experience. The Advaitic intuition, in this regard, could perhaps more appropriately be understood in the perspective of phenomenological intuition (i.e., essence-intuition). The cardinal principle of Husserlian phenomenology is that every primordial object-giving ('dator') intuition is correspondingly 'the source of authority for knowledge.' (The essence-wise insight of phenomenology corresponds to pure essence or 'eidos', the ideal meaning of objectivity in the given context.) In Advaita, however, with its 'practical' interest as the 'Science of Liberation' (*Mokṣa-Śāstra*) and its definite cultural background, intuition no doubt takes on the colour of a firm ethico-spiritual discipline in the shape of *śravaṇa* etc., oriented to the goal of *mokṣa* through self-realization. The focus of Advaitic interest, unlike in the Husserlian, is not primarily fixed on objectivity; the analysis of objectivity would provide only the counter-moment for directing the focus on to subjectivity—its very core.

Coming now to the acclaimed role of intellect *vis-a-vis* intuition in Advaita thought, mere intellectual method of logical reasoning (*tarka*) independent of intuitional basis has been ruled out in the search for essential truths. For mere intellectual reasoning cannot give any new content but can

*In commenting upon the verse under reference, Rāmakṛṣṇa refers to *buddhi* as the means of distinguishment (*buddhyā niṣkṛṣya*), approximating to the sense of 'transcendental reflection'.

only arrange (or re-arrange) materials already at hand. In examining the role of logical reasoning, Śaṅkara points to its necessary instability and inherent shortcomings in the matter of realizing the supreme essence. For such truths as are finally to be obtained through scriptures (*āgamagamya artha*), cannot as such form the subject-matter of independent ratiocination (*svatantratarkāviṣaya*).[6] The subjective (individual) feats of ratiocination move spirally, as it were, round the centre of the empirical content—forming concentric circles but seldom gaining any new ground of experience. It is no doubt true that the logical process of inferring things not evident to our present experience may serve our practical purpose; but in matters of non-empirical import, as in respect of *essences* (phenomenologically speaking) in the region of pure experience, it would prove to be inadequate.

Of course, Śaṅkara does accept the value of reasoning, when it proceeds in the light of authentic experience as embodied in *śruti—āgamānusāri-tarka.*[7] This shows a deeper kind of reflection than the logical, not strictly confined within the limits of formal and external interconnexions of data yielded by sense-experience. Such reflection should rather be concerned with an insight into the inner essence behind the common logico-empirical categories of experience. Even when logical reasoning is necessitated for ascertaining (*niścaya*) the content of intuition, it is to proceed in the light of that very intuition and not as independent of, or contrary to it.[8] Indeed, reasoning independent of intuitional background (conveyed by *Śruti* in the Vedāntic context) is barren—*śuṣka tarka*—and as such is to be avoided. As in phenomenology proper, mediate inference is admitted only as having 'the methodological meaning' of leading us towards that which is to be revealed by direct essential insights relevantly following upon the inferences concerned. The *sūtra*, "*Janmādyasya yataḥ*" is accordingly interpreted not as an instance of inferring *Brahman* from the world of ordered forms and relations but as leading to the truths behind the scriptural texts—*vedāntavākyapradarśanārtham.*

One question may still be raised as to this implicit method of reflective intuition. It is repeatedly stressed, on the one hand, that knowledge concerning realities must conform to relevant objects—*vastutantra*—and as such not be subjectively conditioned by the knowing individual—*puruṣatantra*. And at the same time the course of discipline in the form of hearing etc. is prescribed for the aspirant of truth. How are we then to reconcile these apparently conflicting positions of subjective activity and of objective passivity? The answer may be found in the peculiar status that transcendental essences seem to enjoy. While *revealed* in the essential insight and as such not *created* by knowing activity, they would own validity only as revealed in intuition.

So long as the focal point of the mind reflecting were not reached, relevant essences could hardly be posited. This may analogically be somewhat understood in the light of the manner in which a streak of sun's ray pouring into a room through a hole illuminates the mass of dust particles on its way—those that were so long as good as non-existent to the plain eyes. Thus the Vedāntic practices and injunctions (*vidhi*) would be relevant only in the matter of bringing about the mental focus in stages of higher and higher essentiality; the ideal efficacy of injunction lies in turning the mind to the attitude of transcendental reflection.*

3

Role of *Cit* : Transcendental Subjectivity

Śaṅkara starts with positing the *evident* opposition between subject and object—one is the experiencing cognising principle, the other is the experienced and cognised. However, their duality should not exclude the *empirical* fact of their mutual identification; bare psychological evidence speaks for it. It is a fact of experience that 'I', however subjectively understood, is sometimes spoken of in objective terms. We need not necessarily express *I qua* subjectivity, i.e., as distinguished from object; we also make such statements as 'This is I'. In 'this-*I*'

*To accept *vidhi* in the *Mīmāṃsā* sense of injunction for action would go against the fundamental stand of Advaita that *knowledge* (*jñāna*) is independent of activity on the part of the knower. The injunction that is accepted in Advaita is rather to be interpreted as one of *law* (*niyamavidhi*), as the Vivaraṇa school holds. (cf. *Vivaraṇa* I, p. 3ff.; *Vivaraṇa-prameyasaṅgraha*, p- 3ff).

equation 'this' evidently refer to the bodily-objective locus. And the admittedly subjective factor so far as it is implied by 'I' is not merely referred to an objective locus but is also sought to be *identified* therewith.

Yet, behind such seeming identification of subjectivity and the objective as exemplified in the given statements, the possible subsistence of the two factors in dissociation from each other should be recognized—the substratum (*adhiṣṭhāna*) and the falsely imposed (*adhyasta*) can stand mutually distinguishable, though not *actually* distinguished. The subject in such a situation seems to have no status by itself other than a *functional* one in terms of objective behaviour. However, the said subject-object identification is *seeming*; for the true relation between self and non-self is, after all, one of radical opposition. This opposition is enabled through a transition from the psychological subjectivity of the empirical individual to the *transcendental subjectivity* of pure consciousness (*cit*).[9] And the latter, as Husserl contends, cannot be obtained through the *natural* attitude of empirical psychology; for it is no part of the objective world but is rather the subjective conscious life itself.*

Now the phenomenon of error (*adhyāsa*) indeed provides for Advaita the point of departure from psychological to transcendental subjectivity. As noted in the last section, the phenomenon of error (*adhyāsa*) involving contradiction provides the concrete occasion with which reflection might start. The said erroneous identification of self and non-self is regarded as the commonest confusion in human life and as such forms the chief item of *adhyāsa*. The psychological features (epistemologically relevant at the same time) of agency (*kartṛtva*), cognisership (*pramātṛtva*) etc. constitute different aspects of basically the same confusion. In these cases the supposed subjectivity of consciousness necessarily appears in the objective context. Consequently, the inner being is regarded as objective or non-self quite as much as the body or bodily characteristics.

*Husserl indeed, defines 'transcendental' as 'the quality of that which is consciousness'. (*Vide Encyclopaedia Britannica* Art. on "Phenomenology").

This appearance of one thing in the aspect of another (*anyasya anyadharmāvabhāsa*) is the essential character of the situation of error. Now, in the underlying subjectivity behind the said psychological phenomena is recognized the principle which is *ideally* free from the tinge of objectivity. On the other hand, the objective physico-mental manifold is supposed to make its appearance to this inner subject. Even the empirical ego or '*I*' (*aham*), with all its physico-mental associations and world-involving references, is conceived as presented to a deeper '*I*' which has a presuppositional evidencing character.*

The fundamental presuppositional status of consciousness is signified when it is stated that things whether known or even unknown are in the long run evidenced by the witnessing consciousness.** Here a distinction is evidently drawn between knownness in the ordinary sense and being (transcendentally) evidenced. The ways of knowing (*pramāṇa*) are indeed relevant in the context of knowing a thing. But Advaita would not deny the possible existence of things independent of being cognised by us. Things may be there *for* the subject, even though the latter is not actually cognizant of them by way of valid means of knowing such as perception inference etc. [Of course, the object as *unknown* is explained in terms of the mediating third factor of nescience (*ajñāna*) obtaining between pure evidencing subject and object—its exact character vis-a-vis *cit* being taken up in subsequent section.]

Such recognition of even the *unknown* being evidenced by the witnessing consciousness would exempt it from the standing charge of 'ego-centric predicament' brought against empirical (or psychological) idealism. In the latter, no distinction seems to be drawn between 'to know' and 'to be aware of'. Advaita, however, draws a sharp distinction between the two *levels* of (i) being cognized through the way of knowing and (ii) being evidenced by the witnessing consciousness (*sākṣi-cāitanya*). It

---

*One may compare here the Husserlian position : "The 'I' and 'we' which we apprehend presuppose a hidden 'I' and 'we' to whom they are present" (Husserl, En. Brit. Art.)

**"*Sarvam vastu jñātatayā vā ajñātatayā sākṣicaitanyasya viṣaya eva*", *Vivaraṇa*, I.

would accordingly not be incoherent to admit the uncognized (*ajñāta*) as *transcendentally* evidenced (*sākṣibhāsya*). Such a contention could be possible only from the standpoint of transcendental subjectivity. In this sense Advaita, like the realist, may as well recognise the independent being of *uncognized* object—its relative independence at least. [The distinction of the Advaitic standpoint from the Buddhistic mentalism (*Vijñānavāda*) is here relevant—no transcendental background of subjectivity other than psychic states themselves being admitted in the latter].

To come to a fundamental epistemological tenet of Vedānta, the knowledge-of-object situation is constituted by identification with consciousness (*cit-tādātmya*). On ultimate analysis, some sort of identification or fusion with evidencing consciousness is posited to be at the root of the manifestation of object. Such fusion may be effected either through some mediation (*vyavadhāna*) of the process of valid knowing (*pramāṇavyāpāra*) or without any mediation whatsoever. All objective entities come to be apprehended through the mediation of modes of knowing. The internal organ (*antaḥkaraṇa*) alone—which is at the same time the principle of individuality (*ahaṅkāra*)—is to be revealed independent of any knowing process as such.[10]

Turning again to the Vedāntic notion of self, the Upaniṣads in general and Śaṅkara posit it as the terminus in the ever-deepening series of senses, objects of sense-experience, mind and so on as may be traced in the gradual steps of transcendental reflection.[11] Of course, the analogy of a series should not be taken here to signify that self is just a final term in the series beginning with senses. Self is certainly the innermost as behind all the stages of experience, and behind it nothing further *inner* (*āntara*) is conceivable. Nevertheless it is not a mere *part* of the series but belongs at the same time to a new plane as it were—a transition to a new dimension of being.*

---

*An analogy from mathematics may help us in understanding the position better. Thus, for instance, a geometrical line can conceivably be divided into smaller and smaller sections, till a *point* is reached. Though such points constitute the line as its parts, the point as such also presents a new dimension of its own—a new level of being. For, in the strictly geometrical sense, while a line has only one *dimension* (taking the term not in its wider sense as in the former use), a point has none.

In the case of self as the final 'inner', we need not bring in the parallel of ordinary 'inner' where antecedence and consequence of order in respect of two terms are necessarily presupposed.[12] The enumeration of such a series may have at least the efficacy of bringing home to the unreflective mind the unique character of self—helping the mind which is naturally directed outwards to turn gradually towards the self within.[13] In the Vedāntic emphasis on the non-mundane (*asaṃsāri*) character of self not involved within the continuum of worldly process, the transcendentality of self-subject is all the more clearly brought forward.

4

Cit in the Light of Conscious Act

An analysis of experience, to be truly phenomenological, should no doubt proceed on the implicit assumption that consciousness is of the nature of *act* in the sense of reference-function being constitutive of consciousness. But, then the immediate question would be : can pure consciousness (*cit*), recognised in Advaita to be substantively autonomous, be understood in terms of *act*? It cannot after all be denied that consciousness is actually grasped in its *immanence* (in the phenomenological sense) so far as it is involved within mental states themselves (the point to be developed in the context of perception in the next section). [Under acts 'immanently directed' or 'intentional' experiences immanently related Husserl includes those acts of consciousness which are essentially so constituted "that their intentional objects, when these exist at all, belong to the same stream of experience as themselves."] [14] Now in the aspect of *immanence* alone would it be relevant to speak of consciousness as act, pure or modified.

Phenomenologically speaking, all that may be evident to us is that consciousness is immanently involved in every conscious state as the necessary factor of *evidencing*. Coming to Advaita theory, object is reduced to *vṛtti* which in its turn cannot stand but as evidenced by consciousness. So, object is not taken in its 'transcendence' (in the sense of being real beyond the stream of experience) but is sought to be reduced to consciousness by way of *vṛtti*-mediation. On the level of modalized knowledge (*vṛtti-jñāna*), object-reference by way of *vṛtti* implies the way of being consciously constituted. Such *vṛtti*-mediation is admitted to be present at every level of knowledge, external or internal. Even when *vṛtti* is not produced through the senses—as in the case of internal experience of mental states, for instance—some sort of *vṛtti* besides the evidencing consciousness as such would be necessary to make a state of consciousness possible.[15]

But the question may be raised at this stage : should then consciousness be regarded necessarily as 'functional' in the sense described, or only adventitiously so ? Now, 'function' as it should be understood in the context of evidencing consciousness should first of all be sharply distinguished from certain current uses of the expression. 'Function' may mean, for instance, external activity (on the part of some being or thing), not grounded in the nature of the agent concerned but mechanically or accidentally related to it. There is again the case of "mathematical function" a mathematical system expressing the function of certain symbol, say X, is grounded in the symbol concerned.*

Now, phenomenologically considered—in which sense alone could functionality be admitted of consciousness—'function' is to be understood as grounded in the essence of 'noeses' or those in accordance with which consciousness points to something of which it is the consciousness. What is meant here is not, strictly speaking, the function *of* consciousness but rather—to follow the Husserlian mode of analysis—the very manner in which objective unities of every region of being and of every grade of generality or category are 'consciously constituted'.**

---

*A function is a mathematical system consisting of a set *A* (the range of the independent variable) and a set *B* (the range of dependent variable) and a correspondence which pairs with every element of A some element of *B*.

**According to Husserl, the 'functional problem' is concerned with how 'all fundamental types of possible consciousness and the modifications, fusion, syntheses which essentially belong to them' may be systematically studied 'in their eidetic generality and phenomenological purity'. (*Ideas*, p. 253).

However, Advaita would rather depart from the strictly phenomenological point of view which proceeds with 'eidetic essence' in the form of 'consciousness of'. For in Advaita, the emphasis is shifted from the question of *form*, pertaining to 'consciousness of', to the concrete ground of consciousness itself. So there should be no 'functional problem' as such for Advaita—the problem which no doubt occupies the central position in Husserl's phenomenology,* in which consciousness by itself remains more or less a formal presupposition from the functional point of view. [Of course, even Husserl—somewhat in the Vedāntic fashion—admits that consciousness is not a title-name for 'psychical complexes' but "it is consciousness through and through, the source of all reason and unreason, all right and wrong, all reality and illusion, all value and disvalue, all deed and misdeed."] [16]

Before mentioning the classification of the functional modes of consciousness (so far as consciousness may be said to *have* 'noetic' or meaning function), the *vṛtti-cit* relation should be closely examined. Now, the principle of *sākṣin* in Advaita combines in itself the elements of pure consciousness and of nescience (*ajñāna*)—the latter being there in its unmodified stage. *Cit*—even though involved at the highest stage of immanence within *sākṣin*—nevertheless tends to be distinguished in its autonomous being, although such distinguishment may not reach beyond 'possibility'. But nescience on its part could not similarly be distinguished from the complex of *sākṣin*. And if *sākṣin* is sought to be abstracted in its pure aspect from the said complex, no definite content would remain – such content as may be identified to be nescience *per se*. The relation between *cit* and *vṛtti* has similarly to be understood—*vṛtti* being, on ultimate analysis, nothing but modalized nescience as following from *antaḥkaraṇa*. *Vṛtti* should not be regarded as a definite content in abstraction from the complex of *vṛtti*-evidenced-by-*cit*—which may confirm our approach to *vṛtti* not as pre-existent content which happens to be evidenced by *cit* through mechanical relation but as the functional correlate of *cit*.

**Cf.* "The viewpoint of Function is the Central viewpoint of Phenomenology", *ibid.* p. 252.

There may be two ways in which cognitive consciousness possibly functions—namely, as valid cognition and as pseudo-cognition in the illusory situation. The former is effected through the modalization of internal organ—*antaḥkaraṇa-vṛtti* in the form of the object concerned and the latter through the modalization of nescience—*avidyā-vṛtti*—with illusory object as content. But why at all should a mode other than that of psychic organ be recognised? This entails a detailed treatment of the problem of error and of the determining principle of nescience (*avidyā* or *ajñāna*) in that context (see later).

Chapter VI

ADVAITA METAPHYSIC OF EXPERIENCE

Phenomenological Reconstruction

5

Analysis of Perception

A critique of experience proper should proceed right from the fact of perception-of-object. The element of evidencing cognition (*sākṣātkāri-jñānatva*) is generally recognised to characterize the form of knowing called *pratyakṣa.** So far as perception is primarily *sense-perception,* the Nyāya definition of *pratyakṣa* as 'knowledge originating from sense-object relation' (*indriyārtha-sannikarṣotpannam jñānam*) is commonly accepted. But a mere objectivistic (not to speak of naturalistic) explanation of the situation is not enough for Advaita; an explanation of the same from a *transcendental* standpoint is sought to be introduced.

To start with, the question of the object of perception as independently existent is shifted in Advaita—as in any avowedly transcendental philosophy—to the question of the object as *meant* or 'intended', or in other words, of consciousness being 'intentionally related' to the object**. The latter is necessarily to be understood in terms of *reference* of the knowing subject;

---

*Such broad characterization of perception is basically accepted by some other systems of Indian philosophy too. According to the Prābhākara, it is "*sākṣātkāri-vijñānatva*"; the Bhāṭṭa defines it thus: "*Sākṣātpratītiḥ pratyakṣam*".

**While Kant was connerned with the transcendental analysis of objectivity rather than with the object *per se* ('Ding-an-sich'), Husserl went further—the existentially posited object being 'bracketed' with a view to phenomenological reduction. Advaita resembles Husserl rather that Kant in its concern not so much for a logical-transcendental analysis of objectivity in its strictly *formal* character as such but rather for 'essence' in the realm of pure experience.

and this may correspond in Advaita to the factor of *vṛtti*. The modes of presentation of object, external or internal, are sought to be reduced to the modifications of internal organ (*antaḥkaraṇa-vṛtti*). There seems to be no apparent reason why object should be revealed to, and in identification with, the knowing consciousness so different from it. The case could hardly be explained as one of *accidental* co-existence of object and consciousness ('compresence', as S. Alexander would put it). Such 'compresence' may be an external description of the situation but would miss the essence thereof. To regard consciousness as standing in an exclusive region of its own and focusing, as it were, on the object like a 'torchlight' would hardly improve the matter, because no common point of contact between the two could be shown thereby.

Now it has to be admitted, in a situation of subject knowing the object, the knowledge concerned may be evident in the context of respective psychic modes alone. The given object brings into effect the respective modification of psychic organ; it provides, on the other hand, an occasion for consciousness implicit in the background to be explicit. There could be no manifestation of consciousness *in vacuo* except in the context of object providing the occasion for consciousness to be manifest. So the object of perception is regarded in Advaita epistemology as generating the corresponding psychic mode and serving at the same time as the medium of manifestation of consciousness.[17] (Unlike the object of perception, the *inferred* object would lack in the capacity to modify internal organ in its own form; for the object concerned can enter the inferential judgment only *indirectly*—by way of a series of connecting grounds. The actual object would not be present to form the corresponding mode; only the *existence* of object can be envisaged so that the object in concrete would actually remain unrevealed.)*

The internal organ (*antaḥkaraṇa*) (whose precise status will be shown later) is indeed there as the mediating factor,

*The distinction between the two types of *ajñāna*, viz., *asattāpādaka* and *abhānāpādaka*,—one pertaining to mere existence of object and the other to its actual manifestation—has been formulated in later Advaita works; inference can remove only the existential nescience.

relating consciousness to object; the latter gets associated with the former—with the result that it assumes modification (*vṛtti*) accordingly. Through this association with the internal organ alone does the object derive its capacity for reflecting consciousness. So a perceptible object should have the capacity to modify the internal organ in its own form, the latter in its turn acting as the medium for actual and specific manifestation of consciousness and thereby defining the same.[18] Further, consciousness even seems to refer direct to the external object as 'out there.' That means, the object of perceptual experience takes on the form of the object *intended* as through the modification of internal organ— *vṛtti* distinguishes the object *intended* from one not so. To put the situation in more concrete terms, consciousness may be spoken of not merely as pertaining to, but as 'limited' (*avacchinna*) by, the object concerned.*

The mode of consciousness in the form of cognising subject (*pramātṛ-caitanya*) may be more evident than the so-called *object-form* of consciousness shown above. However, this distinction of the two defining modes of consciousness should not be carried too far. For the same internal organ, connected to both the poles of cognizing subject (*pramātā*) and of the object cognised, effects in a dual manner the apparent limitation (*avaccheda*) of consciousness. As the medium of manifestation is at the root the same, the two apparent forms in which consciousness seems to be manifest, viz., as object and as cogniser, need not be taken as mutually disconnected.[19]

Further the question arises: how to account for the factor of agenthood or *my-ness* in knowing? The unique character of agenthood (*kartṛtva*) belongs originally to *antaḥkaraṇa*; and from agenthood would follow the quality of *cognisership*, i.e., being the agent of knowing act—a quality that evidently cannot belong to the object of cognitive act. Thus as internal organ is itself characterised by the quality of agenthood, the consciousness defined by it should naturally assume the character of

*The *object-form* of consciousness (*viṣaya-caitanya*) as posited in some later Advaita works (e.g., *Vedānta-paribhāṣā*), seems to suggest a kind of 'objective consciousness'. But such 'objective consciousness' would hardly be intelligible, consciousness necessarily meaning something subjective.

cognisership."[20] However, the apparent forms of object and of cogniser pertaining to consciousness need not be taken in abstraction from each other; they are rather to be regarded as two *moments* of the self-same act of consciousness—*intending* an object and *intended* by the subject.

It may be noted in conclusion that the character of 'immanence' (in the phenomenological sense) would follow from the account of perceptual experience so far given. In the Advaita theory of perception, object is reduced to *vṛtti*, which in its turn cannot stand but as evidenced by consciousness. So the object is not taken in its 'transcendence' (in the sense of being *real* beyond the stream of experience) but is sought to be reduced to consciousness by way of *vṛtti*-mediation. That would not, of course, mean that the perception of object is to be regarded as in any way *internal* ; rather the realistic position of the independent reality of things and the externality of sense-perception is shared. But from the *transcendental* point of view, the object as relevant to experience is taken to be in some *alogical* relation of identity with consciousness. Identity with consciousness no doubt proves ultimately to be the essential import of objectivity; but such identity again is recognised to be something alogical and as such, false (*ādhyāsika*).* Further implications of the Vedāntic analysis of perceptual experience would be clarified when illusory experience is analysed and the unique role of *ajñāna* in the Vedāntic metaphysic of experience explained (q.v. sections 6 & 7).

6

Analysis of Illusory Experience

By an appeal to common-sense Advaita contends that illusory perception is a *positive* fact and as such cannot be explained away as something merely negative. It maintains at the same time that though the object of illusory perception is a presented content, it lacks the character of the object of normal

*Husserl too, while stating that in 'immanent perception' perception and the thing perceived essentially constitute "an unmediated unity, that of a single concrete cogitatio", admits at the same time that the two are "in principle and of necessity not really and essentially one and united", *vide Ideas*, p. 124, p. 130.

perception. For unlike the latter, it does not possess the relatively stable character. So a type of knowing, different from valid knowing (*pramāṇa*), is to be admitted. Such knowing need not be incompatible with the absence of relevant knowledge, though it would possess at the same time some of the common characteristics of valid cognition. They are : (i) the capacity for occasioning retrospective cognition in the form of "I know'; (ii) subsequently generating wish etc.; (iii) causing subsequent mental traces and dispositions (*saṃskāra*). Even in illusory experience referentiality would be there; only here the 'noetic' or meant content would not cohere with the content of *standard* experience (in the self-same situation).

Now the genesis of illusory experience cannot be explained with reference to senses as in valid cognition. The illusory object is a complex, of which the substratum (indicated by *this*) is in direct contact with sense-organ; but the latter could hardly account for the peculiar unstable character of the illusory content. For such content, though seemingly given, is nothing short of a 'construction' in the locus concerned; and senses cannot go beyond the limit of the given. Neither could such illusion be due to mental traces, because the latter may give rise to memory and not to perception; nor could it be caused directly by any defect (*doṣa*) in the medium of experience, because such defect by itself would not have any capacity for producing a content as such. So the additional factor of *nescience* (*avidyā*) has to be postulated as that which effects the phenomenon of illusory perception.

The supposed nescience, again, may assume two forms, viz., of object (*vastu*) and of knowledge (*vṛtti*)—under two respective conditions. The object of illusory cognition may be taken as the objectified modification of nescience ; the objective unity of the content of illusion represents a fusion of the locus (*this*) and the misplaced content—the latter ascribing (falsely) a specific character to the former. The unity of consciousness in the aspect of illusory cognition would, on the other hand, represent meaning-consciousness in this context. Objectivity may assume unity through fusion of the false content with the real locus, while similar unity would characterize the consciousness involved in the said objective situation. In the latter case, the double modes of *antaḥkaraṇa* and of *avidyā* get fused into one apprehension.[21] *

Now this description of illusory experience in terms of *ajñāna* and its twofold modes may well be understood phenomenologically. The phenomenon of illusory perception does not represent a form of experience to be treated as altogether different from common experience. The phenomenological explanation in terms of 'intentionality' should also apply here, as in normal experience. Accordingly, illusory experience as much as normal experience may be considered in its *noetic* phase, i.e. as harbouring in itself a *meaning*. In this sense, illusion should be viewed in the light of the 'noetic-noematic structure' of 'intentional' experience—of the ways of being conscious so far as they pertain to illusory experience.

Thus, on the one hand, an illusory experience—its illusoriness granted—would mean a definite *content* in the object of illusion—its 'noematic' content. On the other hand, the *meaning* precisely as it lies 'immanent' in experience—in the pure form of experience itself—constitutes the 'noetic' correlate; the latter may be represented in the Vedāntic terminology by *avidyā-vṛtti*. It should, however, be noted in connexion with the Vedāntic analysis that unlike in Husserl's phenomenology, the noetic phase with the corresponding noematic content are not considered in dissociation from the real object (as in Phenomenology,) but rather in the context of the latter. [Of course, the implicit admission of the *transcendental* background of *sākṣi-caitanya* is there.]

However, a sharp line of distinction is drawn between the illusory (*prātibhāsika*) and the empirical (*vyāvahārika*) levels of knowledge, there being some sort of 'asymmetrical' relation between the two (in respect of validity). The typical Advaita concept of 'inexplicability' (*anirvācyatva*) here comes into view—it refers to the *seeming* objectivity that pertains to the content of false perception. The marked difference of such content from

---

* *Vivaraṇa* gives a detailed analysis of illusory perception in terms of nescience-mode (*avidyā-vṛtti*), which acts as the condition (*upādhi*) in effecting apparent knowledge (*jñānābhāsa*)—taking as object the false content (such as silver in the nacre-silver illusion). cf. *Vivaraṇa*, I, p. 29.

that of valid cognition is that here the subjective (psychical) element of image is mixed up with the objective element of percept. Psychologically viewed, the situation of error (*adhyāsa*) means the confusion of perceived content with remembered image, as Śaṅkara defines it—"*Smṛtirūpaḥ paratra pūrvadṛṣṭāvabhāsaḥ*". Even accepting the image aspect of the content, Advaita never takes illusory perception as a simple case of remembering. [Indeed *Anirvacanīyakhyāti* rejects *Akhyāti*, so far as the latter wrongly introduces the element of remembering (*smṛti*) in perceptual experience.] The experience of falsity is not merely a case of negative non-discrimination (*vivekāgraha*), as *Akhyātivāda* urges, but it is characterized by the presence of *positive* content (*bhāvavastu*).

Indeed the content *qua* content is never denied in the Advaita view; what is denied is the character of *reality* as referring to a real spatio-temporal context. In false perception, the object on primary reflection is found to be lacking the character of *reality* that pertains to the object of *valid* perception. Accordingly, the *Anyathākhyāti* view that the content of false cognition is characterized by reality, though 'transferred' from the *actual* object, is not entertained. So, to explain the appearance of false object as a sort of 'extended' perception of the *real* object at some other point of space and time seems plainly to contradict the experience of false object in the locus at hand. The alleged existence of false object as 'distant' in space (*deśāntarīya*) and in time (*kālāntarīya*) goes contray to the evident feeling of presentedness of the false object before us. Further, the element of (distinguishable) association, felt reflectively, between the real and the unreal is also ignored in the Naiyāyika explanation.

It should be noted here that even the said reality-character need not be treated as pertaining to an order different from the immanent region of pure experience. For the false content itself can indeed be viewed *qua intended* (in the act of consciousness as represented by *avidyā-vṛtti*). Accordingly, existentiality or reality should rather be viewed as immanently involved in the essentiality of the content without necessarily transcending to a reality *external* to the region of pure intuition. In this case the *intended* object essentially turns upon the very act rather than subsisting by itself, as the content of valid knowledge does.

Consequently, such *false* content seems to possess a 'noematic' character of an *intermediate* type—embodying reference, but not to reality. As such it may properly be regarded as belonging to the tertiary order of the 'inexplicable' (*anirvācya*).

Further, the typical but significant mode in the forms of *I* or ego (*ahaṅkāra-vṛtti*) should be considered in this context. The modalization of consciousness in the form of *I* appears to be characterized by a peculiar indefiniteness; it cannot be treated as an ordinary mode of consciousness that implies some definite content by itself. In this respect the I-mode seems rather to share the character of false perception, although such mode is regarded as *empirical* (*vyāvahārika*) like any case of normal experience.

Of course, the ground for ascribing I-mode to the region of nescience rather than to that of valid modes is not far to seek. It is evident that the mode in the form of *I* does not stand alone but necessarily accompanies some modification in object-form. As such, the I-mode is dependent upon the object of cognition although *I* posits itself as *other* than the latter.[22]* Once it is recognised that *I* and object are revealed in cognition simultaneouly—*I* not being evident in isolation,—the question would arise if two co-existing modes could be of the same order of valid cognition. For, the simultaneous presence of two definite contents of consciousness seems to be an evident absurdity in experience. So the seeming forms of *I* in consciousness, having no definite content of its own, should be ascribed to the region of *nescience*.

Now, if I-mode belong to the order of nescience, the conditioning defect (*doṣa*) would have to be indicated—the latter being an 'efficient' condition in the situation of error. Here nescience itself has been pointed out as the said condition; unlike in ordinary error, the defect is not adventitious (*āgantuka*) but necessary. The (relatively) constant factor of individual nescience (in the shape of *antaḥkaraṇa*) rather than the contingent factor of variable *doṣa* is here in view. And as nescience itself

*In Nyāya philosophy too, self as equivalent to *I* is admitted to be knowable only in conjunction with the specific qualities abiding in self—"*Dharmādharmāśrayaḥ adhyakṣa viśeṣaguṇayogataḥ*".

serves, on ultimate analysis, as the ground of all empirical use and practice (q.v. section 7), the mode issuing directly from nescience should be regarded as empirical (*uyāvahārika*); in other cases nescience-modes would be purely illusory (*prātibhāsika*). (Indeed psychic organ itself could become *object* for the evidencing consciousness only by way of I-mode.)[23]

7

Principle of Nescience (*Ajñāna/Avidyā*)

In a philosophy wedded to subjectivity, the concept of Nescience stands for the principle of objectification—the prime *alogical* factor that hinges on to unobjective consciousness. The motive behind the Advaitic treatment of erroneous perception is no doubt to introduce the indeterminable principle of nescience (*ajñāna*). Proofs—perceptual and inferential (also postulational)—are advanced by Advaita for showing nescience as a *positive* principle. *Ajñāna* does imply something more than mere absence of knowledge, although it may *prima facie* seem that *ajñāna* could bear a meaning only as implying the negation or absence (*abhāva*) of knowledge. But negation in relation to conscious evidencing (rather than to things) presents a unique character.

On the evidence of such judgment as "I am ignorant", the negativity of the alleged 'non-knowledge' would involve a plain contradiction. It is argued that the perception of negation necessitates the perception of the negatum (*pratiyogi*) concerned in the self-same locus.* But to follow the same analysis in the case of the felt absence of *knowledge* (as explicitly stated in such judgment as 'I do not know') would lead to a contradiction. For that would mean the subsistence of knowledge and of its absence in the very same locus, the self, at the same time—

*Of course Advaita, unlike Nyāya, substitutes for perception (*pratyakṣa*) another *pramāṇa*, viz., *anupalabdhi*, for the knowledge of the so-called negative facts. (The apprehension of *ajñāna* is a case of perception, according to Advaita, though of a higher order than that of sense-perception.) However, the knowledge of the positive counter-correlate (*pratiyogī*) is admitted in Advaita too as necessary in *anupalabdhi*.

and that means an evident contradiction. So the alleged absence of knowledge has to be understood differently than ordinary negation (*abhāva*). (The case of *suṣupti* may be referred to in this context.)

The common process of negation is directed object-ward. The ignorance as to a particular object is one thing, while the perception of the ignorance itself is another. In the former, consciousness is direted to an objective situation, while in the latter it is directed to a moment within itself that tends to counter its own referentiality. Such moment, it seems, would neutralize the very evidencingness of consciousness, being itself the agent of obscuration (in respect of consciousness). Thus, nescience as the positive (*bhāvarūpa*) obscuring principle has for its locus and its object the self-same principle of consciousness—*samānāśrayaviṣayam bhāvarūpam ajñānam.**

However, in the zeal for establishing nescience as *positive*—so that it may not be confused with mere absence (*prāgabhāva*) of knowledge—the *raison d'etre* of the principle is not to be overlooked. To raise the issue of positivity to a *metaphysical* status would ultimately amount to the position of 'Consciousness *plus* Nescience' (the latter in that case proving to be as much an independent principle as *Prakṛti* of Sāṅkhya philosophy). But such a position may lead to serious difficulties. How to explain the primary alogical connexion between *Cit* and *Ajñāna*? Another nescience-principle would be necessitated. [In Sāṅkhya philosophy, an original alogism (*anādi aviveka*) between *Puruṣa* and *Prakṛti* has indeed been posited to explain the primary association of the two.] That would only involve a confusion of categories.

Leaving aside the realistic-metaphysical orientation, the essential status of nescience should be considered. Nescience *per se* is hardly to be felt; *ajñāna* would stand as indefinite, were it taken in abstraction from the complex formed through association with *Cit*. To look more closely into the relation of

---

*The positivity (*bhāvarūpatva*) of *ajñāna* is proved also inferentially. The proof through inference proceeds indirectly, by showing the characteristics of valid knowledge (*pramāṇajñānam*), which cancels erroneous knowledge. Cf. *Vivaraṇa*, I, p. 13; *Vivaraṇa-prameya-Saṅgraha*, p. 17f.

ajñāna to *cit.*, it can be expressed as one of *function* to essence (of substance). It is an inseparable relation—one that may subsist between, say the burning capacity of fire and fire itself. The metaphysical phase of the position is shown thus : *Māyā* should exist potentially in Brahman, having no reality of its own independent of the latter and to be inferred from the effects following from itself; thus *Māyā* is neither to be identified with Brahman nor is it in essence independent of it.[24]

This brings us to the concept of 'indefinability' (*anirvācyatva*) as a third category other than reality and unreality. In erroneous situation the generic substratum ('this') stands behind the false perception and the opposing right cognition as well. It is the apprehension of the specific content in the generic essence (of the given locus) that removes the false percept. This shows that error necessarily appears on the substratum—"*sādhiṣṭhāno bhramaḥ*", and the content pertaining to it is rejected subsequently as unreal. The correction of false cognition does involve not merely the rejection of the false content but also the right apprehension of the substratum in its true (specific) character. So the complex situation of error involves the substratum (*adhiṣṭhāna*), in which alone the specific character of the given object is to be perceived—and only such perception can finally counter the false one. As such, the erroneous situation could hardly be regarded as simply unreal (*asat*) or 'zero' (*śūnya*). The unreality may be spoken of it only as differentiating it from the real (*sadvyāvṛttimātram*); in order to emphasize its non-real character alone the 'indefinable' may be spoken of as 'unreal'.[25] In respect of ideal autonomy independent of the substratum, the false content may practically be looked upon as unreal or 'nothing' (*śūnya*).[26]

The reality of the substratum thus stands on a level different from that of the appearing content. Consequently, the question of contradiction between the two would not arise from the alogical relation holding between them. The substratum serves as the background on which the false content appears rather than as the factor countering the latter. It is the *specific* character of the substratum which alone is capable of countering the false content. As to the cognizance of nescience as such, *ajñāna* stands revealed to transcendental consciousness; the latter alone enables *ajñāna* to be evidenced at all and in no way does cancel it. And hardly is nescience *per se* conceivable apart from being evidenced—a point already referred to. So nescience is taken as necessarily evidenced by transcendental consciousness. Even if it be contended in doubt (though such doubt would be untenable, as already noted) that the false appears *in vacuo* without a positive support behind it, the *transcendental* support in pure consciousness for a phenomenon of erroneous perception could hardly be denied.

Viewed in the light of an "essentialistic" analysis, transcendental consciousness would prevail on ultimate analysis—even when all floating essences in the region of pure experience were dismissed. Pure consciousness is the final essence which cannot be superseded by any further essence in pure intuition. It not only stands all cancellation but is also the ultimate presupposition of all cancelling acts of consciousness.[27]

The modalized aspect of consciousness alone, and not pure consciousness as such, stands to the corresponding modalized nescience in a relation of necessary contradiction. Due to the distinction in level between pure consciousness and its modalized form in cognition a relation of compatibility — rather than one of contradiction — should subsist between consciousness and nescience. Consequently, it would not be a contradiction to maintain that nescience *abides* in consciousness.[28]

Now, nescience may be regarded in broad stand for *objectivity* as hanging on to unobjective consciousness. In this respect, the concept of *ajñāna* seems to come close to the Kantian conception of 'object in general' — the latter alone confers upon empirical concepts in general the relation to object or objective reality. In the Kantian theory, however, 'object in general' is posited just as a logical postulate implied in *a priori* reflection. *Ajñāna* in Advaita, on the other hand, is not to be understood merely as a formal concept but rather as the concrete implicate of pure experience.* The cognizance of the very presence of nescience is grounded in the evidencing

*In later dialectical Advaita, however, the *formal* aspect of *ajñāna* rather than the phenomenological is emphasised.

consciousness. What the formal approach, either by way of inference or by way of postulation (*arthāpatti*), may assure us is the *formal* character of nescience as other than negative (*abhāvav-yāvṛtti*) or as positive, but cannot by itself evidence the pure content that is nescience.[29]

That *ajñāna* is not a mere logical category may be more evident if we consider how it could be traced from the level of objective experience in degrees of generic essentiality. *Ajñāna* in its pure essence is to be intuited on the transcendental purified level of experience alone. This is suggested by the state of dreamless sleep (*suṣupti*), wherein the unmodified mass of *ajñāna* stands evidenced by the evidencing consciousness. So far as the prior stages of normal and illusory waking experience and of dream are concerned, *ajñāna* is certainly present, but not *qua* *ajñāna*. In case of *empirical* ignorance some reference, explicit or implicit, to this or that object would be there; whereas in the state of *suṣupti* alone could nescience be apprehended in its generic essence. However vague, the efficacy of such nescience-in-general for effecting memory should be recognised, so far as it can yield the impression of *total* ignorance. In error the nescience-content is only retrospectively posited, so far as it is recognised that the actual object were not known. In the intermediate region of normal experience, however, the meaning of nescience changes and nescience is recognizable there, if at all, only as signifying 'function' of consciousness.

Now, on ultimate analysis, *ajñāna* could be taken to represent the functional aspect of Consciousness. The various modalities of Function (in gerenal), in varying degrees of generality, constitute the world of experience. *Ajñāna* (or *Avidyā*), viewed as function in relation to pure consciousness, should represent *Reference in general*; and as such it should stand on the same level as evidencing consciousness itself. As modalized nescience in the form of modifications (*vṛtti*) of internal organ correspond to modalized consciousness, so unmodalized nescience would correspond to unmodalized consciousness, i.e. *sākṣi-cit.*

The relation that nescience-in-general may be said to bear to evidencing consciousness is to be closely considered. In a possible relation (if at all it could properly be spoken of as *relation*) of *free* association alone can evidencing consciousness and Reference or Function in general share the same transcendental level. Advaita defines such a possible relation with the help of the category of *upādhi* or free association. The latter signifies a relation which is not necessary but *free*—a relation which however is rather concomitant with the essence though not contingent to it. On the path of transcendental reflection, nescience is revealed as necessary, rather than accidental, correlate of consciousness—a status roughly implied by the notion of *quality* (*viśeṣaṇa*). But at the height of such reflection, when the level of the evidencing consciousness (*sākṣi-cit*) itself might be reached, the possible relation should rather be represented by *upādhi* in place of quality (*viśeṣaṇa*).* Thus, on ultimate analysis, the status of nescience should mean the generic (functional) correlate to which pure consciousness remains freely associated. Projecting the essence of this situation on a universal *cosmic* level, we come upon the *Paribhāṣā* extension (as noted in Ch. IV) of the *viśeṣaṇa-upādhi* distinction in respect of *Māyā-Caitanya* relation, thus formulating the ingenious distinction between *Īśvara* and *Īśvara-Skāṣin*. It is the latter, and not the former (called *Parameśvara* by the author—not too unambiguously), which marks the onto-religious embodiment of the highest point of transcendental reflection.**

*See discourse on "*Sākṣin*" (Bh. IV).

**It is interesting to note here how Husserl comes up with a broadly comparable situation, following up his radical method of epoché or suspending of world-belief. In introducing the problematic concept of "transcendental reflection" (cf. *Erste Philosophie*, Second Part, a 34), Husserl poses the intriguing question of the theoretic possibility of the non-being of every 'thing-like transcendence' (in relation to the region of 'purified consciousness')—that it is thinkable that this world could no longer exist having only 'presumptive reality'. Of course, for Husserl, such a possibility of 'world-denial' would never amount to a metaphysical statement. Within the perspective of the radically exercised epoché, the world is 'not vanished'; it would rather stand purely as correlate of transcendental subjectivity, imparting to the world all its 'meaning of being'. So the real accent in this apparent world-nullification is not on any nihilistic or acosmistic position, but rather on the transcendental consciousness, standing 'above' the *natural* world, in its 'world' constituting' autonomy. One could read this whole model of thinking as a

At this stage, the ultimate position of *ajñāna* as *function* in respect of consciousness may be reviewed. It has been noted that there need not be any dualism of essence and function—the latter having no independent status apart from the former. Function *qua* function would rather abide in essence and as such effect the *seeming* activity in the latter.[30] The question of dualism may arise only at the lower level of modifications from *Māyā-śakti*—a level where the succeeding stages derived from the primal Function come to be posited as *independent.* The empirical world of things and beings comes within this region of modifications of the primal function of *Cit* and as such takes on a seeming independence. But even though tending to subsist independent of the primal Essence (*i.e.*, *Cit*), the functional modifications could not by themselves claim substantive autonomy. Here again the category of inexplicability (*anirvācyatva*), as already explained comes into play.

8

Grades Of Reflection

The comprehension of essences in gradual steps within the region of pure experience may be carried out through the corresponding stages of dissociation of the essential correlates of consciousness from the relevant empirical complexes. Thus, to begin with, at the stage of illusory perception nescience appears to subsist in a contingently modalized form as occasioned by extrinsic factors of 'defect' etc. At the other end, however, nescience may possibly be intuited in its generic nature—as in the stage of deep sleep—or better, in enlightened meditation (*samādhi*). Indeed the whole process of approaching the ultimate essence of consciousness might become intelligible in the light of 'grades of reflection'. The higher the grade of

---

phenomenological translation of the notion of the *anirvācya māyic* nature of the world, conceived in its totality, as a *transcendental* (not *vyāvahārika*) situation in respect of *Sākṣin* (more appropriately, *Īśvara-sākṣin*), to whom the total reality of the saṃsāric world would be presented as a *phenomenon*—the entire structure of *jagat* being created by *Īśvara* through free act (in respect of *Māyā-upādhi*). Only phenomenology, strictly speaking, would hardly move on to the onto-religious level of Godhead.

reflection, more in purity the ideal essence would be grasped—through more and more distinguishment of the corresponding nescience-correlates, in which the essence possibly remains involved in the various stages of association. In this manner a stage may *ideally* be reached where the innermost essence could be grasped in its purity, along with the corresponding nescience in its generic character. For such apprehension of nescience in the pure generic form would at the same time reveal it as essentially dependent on Consciousness.*

Indeed, the *raison d'etre* of Vedāntic reflection may be indicated in the progressive apprehension of *pure* essence within the region of consciousness in steps of de-objectification. Correspondingly proceeds *distinguishment*—progressively clearer and more generic—of what may be regarded as the *intentional* correlates of consciousness. At the unreflective stages of waking and of dream, the subject-pole of experience would remain hardly distinguished from the objective correlate—the region of nescience, in larger or smaller degree, within the region of individual consciousness. At the stage of *samādhi*—and imperfectly in *suṣupti* too—the essence of self or consciousness may be restored in its native subjectivity with the denial of the 'other' that has been hitherto prevailing prior to that stage; even the act of denial itself stands to be denied therein. As the essences evident in subjectivity are grasped in progressive dissociation from the manifold of objective presentations, the preceding phases of seeming obscuration and objectification of pure subjectivity, i.e., the corresponding *ajñāna*-counterparts of consciousness, are also recognised as false. In this process of grasping the essential (and the authentic) and rejecting the inessential (and the inauthentic) the ultimate essence of subjectivity could possibly be reached — and therein alone could be realized the truth of all the stages.

Thus the said 'grades of reflection' would imply levels of identification of pure consciousness (*cit*) and nescience in

*Cf. K. C. Bhattacharyya, *Studies in Vedantism*, p. 16f. Bhattacharyya, however, proceeds with the conception of "grades of existence", holding between subject and object, while I prefer to proceed rather in the line of "grades of reflection".

different degrees. And what is empirically as well as transcendentally the most significant stage of such identification is, broadly speaking, that of *mind* (*antaḥkaraṇa*). It marks the first step of descent, as it were, from evidencing consciousness, where there can be reference to the 'other' but not the slightest amalgamation with it. Mind, which stands for various activities of thinking, feeling, perceiving etc., embodies such a stage of amalgamation. Here the principles of pure consciousness and non-consciousness (*acit*) together constitute, as it were, a close fusion (*cidacidgranthi*). The mind-principle indeed plays a cardinal role in the explanation of the features, which though linked to subject, fall short of subjectivity pure. It stands mediating between the two distinct poles of subjectivity and object; and without this mediation the fluctuations in our knowledge of objects could hardly be explained. The mere presentation of object within the field of one's perception may not necessarily amount to cognition; for, the third factor of *attention* (or 'interest') would be further entailed—a factor evidently exercised through *mind*.[31]

Now, mental processes would mean hardly anything if they are not subjective. The mental and the subjective seem to be for all practical purposes equivalent. Still even in our mental introspection a fringe of pure consciousness may be felt as involved within, and yet transcending, mental states themselves. Whether the fringe is taken into account or not, subjectivity is commonly accepted to be valid in the form of 'individuality' alone. To put it otherwise, only through an *alogical* identity with such features of mind as agency, enjoyership etc. pure consciousness may assume the worldly (*saṃsāri*) or empirical character.[32] After all, subjectivity and mind need not be taken as two absolutely different entities related together; for then the relation between the two might as well lapse at any stage.

A mere contingent relation of two mutually independent distincts does not seem to hold between consciousness and mind. For apart from consciousness, mind would be an absurdity in experience. Consciousness in the empirical context stands necessarily linked to the mind-principle, taking on thereby the form of *individuality*. The fusion of pure consciousness with mind, responsible for the usage of self as mind, marks too deep a stratum for the individual to be normally ignored. Even in the state of deep sleep, there would be no absolute cessation of connection with mind-principle; the latter only remains in a 'potent' state as it were. In fact mind and consciousness should be as much inseparable in experience as the light falling on an object would be indistinguishable from the latter, After all, through the medium of mind alone subjectivity gets more and more involved within the region of objects and thus takes its active share in the empirical world of things and beings.[33]

So, mind need not be taken as a solid platform for subjectivity to set its foot on; rather, it is *transitive* in character. Grades of essentiality may be implied by the fourfold functional modes (*vṛtti*) of mind corresponding to the fourfold phases of psychic organ (*antaḥkaraṇa*), viz., *manas*, *citta*, *ahaṅkāra* and *buddhi*. Of these, the faculty of critical intelligence (*buddhi*) marks the highest moment of mentality and approximates most to the essence of subjectivity.* As Śaṅkara remarks, the principle of *buddhi*, by virtue of its 'natural transparency and proximity', reflects the light of consciousness—the "light" said to pervade the different levels of the psycho-physical complex of the individual. Next to critical intelligence it is the associational level of mind (*mamas*) that reflects pure consciousness through its association with *buddhi*. Further, through association with *manas* again can sense-organs reflect consciousness, till finally even the body as invariably associated with sense-organs would get fused with transcendental consciousness.

At the bottom Advaita seems to start with the dim subjectivity on the sub-psychic perceptual level of the *body*, which is *felt* as subject ('I-body') in relation to the physical environment, or of "bodily subjectivity". [Here 'body' is not taken merely in the *naturalistic* sense of a bare psysical entity, a thing

**Buddhi* has often been used by Śaṅkara in the broad sense of 'mind'. But he also makes express distinction between *buddhi* and *manas* as two distinct levels—more in line with the Sāṅkhya metaphysic of experience. (The later Advaita prefers to take them simply as different functions of the self-same principle, overlooking their respective grades of essentiality).

among things, but also as singularly *felt* from within to be one's own.]* This may be followed by the series of media—more and more subtle—for the manifestation of consciousness, till the higher stage of 'critical intelligence' (*buddhi*) were reached. The nodal point of *buddhi*, inalienably involving consciousness, seems to be rather hard to resolve. As Śaṅkara remarks, even the wise one who can distinguish self from non-self has to yield to the primal illusion of taking critical intelligence as the very essential self itself.[34] It is an illusion which is prior to all transcendental confusions and is at the very root of empirical consciousness. Thus by way of gradual associational link with *buddhi* downwards, the whole physico-mental system of the individual comes to partake of the very character of consciousness and as such gets fused with the latter.

This gradual fusion of transcendental consciousness with the common features of personality may be understood in the light of a close analysis of experience. Thus, to start with the higher stage, critical intelligence marks the self-conscious level where the nature and content of experience could be ascertained. Through critical intelligence, the subject may *own* the odd mass of objective data that should enter into the realm of experience, by way of organizing the former. At the associational level of mind, however, the contents of experience would merely be received and assembled; and upon those contents does intellect work. Though the sense of egoity and individuation (*asmitā*) may already be present at the associational level, it is the higher *critical* stage of intellect proper (*buddhi*) which could strictly be regarded as *apperceptive*. Again, mind itself would depend upon sense-organs to gather objective data from outside; the former can function when the materials brought in by the senses are present. But sense-organs, again, cannot function independent of the body, wherein they abide.

From body to critical intelligence upwards, there is the chain of conditional associations in steps of which subjectivity

*Cf. "The body as externally and internally perceived, as observed and felt may be regarded as the subject in relation to the environment and psychology has to start with this bodily subjectivity", K. C. Bhattacharyya *The Subject as Freedom*, Ch. III.

could be grasped in increasing degrees of purity. The alogical process of fusion with consciousness that starts with the first step of *buddhi*, left to itself, extends down to the level of the body. In the task of retracing, the essential nature of consciousness in its authentic core, the path lies through the reverse process of *dissociation*. Now the individual may be freeing himself through respective grades of reflection from the confusion at the level of body or of senses, nay even of mind. Yet the final vestige of human confusion that takes critical experiencing intelligence as the true subject seems hard to transcend.

Precisely at this point, Advaita (and Sāṅkhya alike) would go on further to posit transcendental consciousness (*sākṣi-caitanya*) as the post-intellect index of transcendental reflection. Indeed the whole vital-mental framework of the individual may ultimately be reviewed in the light of transcendental consciousness. Consequently, the status of mind in relation to bodily activity—particularly in the state of deep sleep—should be considered. Normally at the waking stage the phase of bodily activity of the individual is subordinated to the mental act (cf. "felt body" in K. C. Bhattacharyya). Our vital activities have to undergo the necessary mediation, at least implicit, of mind even when the former appear to be spontaneous—*manodhīnatādarśanāt prāṇavṛtteḥ*.[35]

Of course, the question that in deep sleep the vital function of the body seems to operate, even though the mind is admittedly inactive, has to be met in this connexion. To view phenomenologically such seeming independence of the individual's vital phase from his mind, the apparent cessation of the former should be understood from the point of view of evidencing consciousness rather than of external observer. From the standpoint of the evidencing subject the cognizance of the body may be effected only through the mediation of mind. And mind is admittedly inactive during sleep, which would practically mean that the body would be as good as functionless in relation to individual consciousness.

Here comes into view the theory that whatever exists does so only by virtue of its being evidenced by the subject—viz., *dṛṣṭi-sṛṣṭi-vāda*. Advaita proposes to work out into a full-fledged standpoint what is admittedly shown by dream-experience.[36]

Hence it might be urged, if the being of things is admittedly derived by way of evidencing (or being evidenced), then to be consistent, only two terminal levels of being (*sattā*)—the apparent (*prātibhāsika*) and the transcendental (*pāramārthika*)—should strictly be retained (contrary to the traditional Advaita classification into three types of being).* Unless the existence of things unperceived (*ajñātasattā*) be recognised, there may hardly be a justification for bringing in the intermediate category of the *empirical* (*vyāvahārika*), which is commonly accepted by Advaita. Now, even without forgoing the transcendental standpoint of *dṛṣṭisṛṣṭi*, empirical objectivity need not be denied—in view of the evident difference between the two experiences of waking and of dream in the verdict of empirical consciousness.[35] The object of ordinary cognition cannot certainly be denied empirical validity so far as it can effect empirical use (*vyavahāra*) in the form of consequent activity or reaction, whether positive or negative—*jñānajanyapravṛttinivṛtti*.

The progress in Advaita phenomenology from the level of psycho-physical complex to that of consciousness pure marks the gradual steps of reflection. At the one end the ego is completely embedded and involved in the world of things; and at the other end the ego—if there be any vestige of egoity at all at that stage—is left shorn of attachment to the world. In the former, the belief in the world as self-subsistent stands supreme and even man is reflected upon only within the bounds of the *natural* attitude. In the latter, there is a lapse of interest and belief in the world. *Jiva*—commonly meant by *I* and conditioned by the nescience-correlates of psychic organ, sense-organs and dual bodies, subtle and gross—would broadly correspond to the "world-immersed ego" of the phenomenologist.**

*The *pāramārthika* and the *Prātibhāsika* should, in this sense, imply the two plainly contrary categories of the evidencing and the evidenced respectively; although *prātibhāsika*, strictly speaking, should mean the illusory alone.

**E. Fink points out 'the three egos' as involved in Husserl's Phenomenology : (i) the worldly ego or I, i.e., the natural man; (ii) the epoché-performing ego, the 'observer'; and (iii) the transcendental ego. M. Farber seeks to solve the riddle of correlating the three egos by recourse to "degrees of reflection". Farber, *The Foundation of Phenomenology*, p. 553 f.

So far as the Husserlian steps of the observing withdrawing ("epoché-performing") ego and of the *transcendental* ego are concerned, they both seem to be covered by the principle of *sākṣin* in Advaita. The concept of *sākṣin* primarily indicates 'the theoretical transcendental observer', involving no epistemological *use* in positing the world—theoretical or atheoretical. Yet this may be regarded only as the 'immanent' (*taṭastha*) moment of *sākṣin* where the reference to experience-continuum, though free, would necessarily be present. But besides this 'immanent' phase, a 'transcendent' (*kūṭastha*) moment could also be conceived where consciousness should stand completely self-accomplished.*

So we note in conclusion the acclaimed *transcendent* status (beyond the 'transcendental') pertaining to *Cit*, moving even beyond the culminating point of transcendental reflection. Viewed in the perspective of its possible ultimate status, Cit would not, in final analysis, be confined to the region of pure (or purified) experience, and the structure of essence-possibilities immanent therein; it would rather transcend the region of noetic-noematic meaning (as in the strictly phenomenological analysis). Consciousness is no longer just the "phenomenological residuum", as with Husserl, the limiting precondition of all meanings of being; it is, on the contrary, the very Being, which permeates, and imparts meaning to, all meanings.

Unlike in pure phenomenology, epistemological critique is not the guiding concern in Advaita, nor is the analysis (or description) of objectivity the supreme concern. The Vedāntic analysis of consciousness, on the other hand, never loses the sight of the ontic-existential focus. *Cit* is not merely recognised as the irreducible residuum (on which 'reduction can have no grip', as Husserl observes); it proves rather to be the very ontological source, the ultimate existence-stratum, of all possible essences determining the possible modes and levels of

*It can be relevant to note here, by way of comparison, Husserl's characterization of what he calls the "pure I"—distinguished from empirical subjectivity which belongs to the world—as "a quite peculiar transcendence, a transcendence in immanence". (cf. *Ideas* I. 57).

objectivity. But that is an issue to which we address ourselves in the next part of our study.

1. S. Radhakrishan, *The Vedanta according to Samkara and Ramanuja*, p. 87 (George Allen and Unwin).
2. "*Asya anarthahetoḥ prahāṇāya ātmaikatvavidyāpratipattaye sarve vedāntāḥ ārabhyante*", S. B. B. S., *Adhyāsabhāṣya.*
3. Vide *Vivaraṇa-prameya-saṅgraha*, p. 1ff., according to which the other two are regarded as *phalopakārakāṅga.*
4. *Pañcadaśī*, I. 54.
5. "*Anubhavāvasānatvāt bhūtavastuviṣayatvāt ca...*", S. B. B. S.. I. i. 2.
6. S. B. B. S., II, i 11. and *Bhāmatī* thereon.
7. Ibid
8. Cf. "... *śrutyā eva ca sahāyatvena tarkasya abhyupetatvāt*" S. B. B. S., I. i. 2.
9. Cf. *Pañcadaśī*, VI. 30.
10. "*Avyavadhānena citsaṃsarga eva pratibhāsahetur na jñānavyāpāraḥ*", *Vivaraṇa*, I. p. 61.
11. Cr. "*Sarveṣām eva eṣām paratvena pratipādanam*", S. B. B. S., III. iii. 14.
12. *Pañcadaśī*, VI. 167.
13. S. B. B. S., III. iii. 15.
14. *Ideas, p.* 124.
15. Cf. "*Nā hi vṛttim vinā sākṣiviṣayatvam kevalasākṣivedyatvam, kintu indriyānumānādipramāṇavyāpāram antareṇa śākṣiviṣayatvam*", *Vedāntaparibhāṣā, Ch. I.*
16. Edmund Husserl, *Ideas : General Introduction to Pure Phenomenalogy* (trans. B. Gibson), George Allen and Unwin, p. 251 (subsquently referred to as *Ideas*).
17. Cf. "*Kārakatvavyañjakatvadharmadvaya...*" *Vivaraṇa*, I, p. 84.
18. "*Antaḥkaraṇam hi svasminniva svasaṃsargiṇyapi caitanyābhivyaktiyogyatām āpādayati*", *ibid,, p.* 70.
19. "*Pariṇāmasya ubhayasaṃsargād vyañjakābhedena vyaṅgāvicchedaḥ*", *idem.*
20. Cf. "...*antaḥkaraṇasya kartṛtvāt tadavacchinnaḥ pramātā*", *idem.*
21. Cf. "*Yadyapi antaḥkaraṇavṛttiḥ avidyāvṛttiśca iti dve ime jñāne, tathāpi viṣayādhīnam phalam*", Vidyāraṇya, *Sarvadarśanasaṅgraha.* XVI.
22. Cf. "...*viṣayoparaktasapratiyogikasvabhāvasya ahaṅkārasya* ..", *Vivaraṇa*, I, p. 55.
23. "*Ahamvṛtti-avacchinnamev antaḥkaraṇam caitanyasya viṣayabhāvam āpadyate* ", *idem.*
24. "*Nistattva kāryagamyāsya śaktirmāyāgniśaktivat. Nahi ṣaktiḥ kvacit kaiścit budhyate kāryataḥ purā* ..", *Pañcadaśī, II.* 47.
25. Cf. "*Sadvyāvṛttimātram bhramasya asattvam nāma na śūnyatvam niṣedhapratiyogitvāt* ..", *Vivaraṇa*, p. 38.
26. "*Sarbavādinām sarvam vastu svakāle vartamānamapi vināśād ūrdham śūnyameva* ..", *idem.*
27. *Cf.* "*Sarvabhramāvabhāseṣu ca sākṣicaitanyasya ālambanasya vidyamānatvāt* .. *sākṣi eva adhiṣṭhānam avadhiṣca vidyata* ..", *Vivaraṇa, loc. cit.*; also ".. *kūṭasthāparokṣaikarasacaitanyāvadhiḥ sarvasya vādhaḥ*", *Pañcapādika*, p. 12.

28. "*Sākṣicaitanyasya ca ajñānāvabhāsakatvāt na cidāśrayatvavirodhaḥ*", *Vivaraṇa*, *I*, p, 43.
29. *Ibid.*
30. "*Śaktiḥ iti ātmaparatantratayā ātmanaḥ sarvakāryopādānatvasya nirvodhṛtvam...*" *Pañcapādikā.*
31. "..*yasya avadhāna-anavadhānābhyām upalabdhi-anupalabdhī bhavataḥ tanmanaḥ*" S. B. B. S., II. iii. 32.
32. *Ibid*,
33. S. B., *Bṛh. Up.*, IV. iii.
34. *Idem.*
35. *Vivaraṇa*, p. 58.
36. *Idem.*

PART III

BEYOND PHENOMENOLOGY : THE ONTOLOGIGAL STANDPOINT

Chapter VII

ADVAITA PHENOMENOLOGY RECONSIDERED

From our investigations in the preceding section (Part II) which propose to be broadly phenomenological in character, the inadequacy of the strictly phenomenological standpoint in attempting a complete representation of the Advaitic metaphysic of experience may prove to be evident. The present discourse would not permit a closer review of the standpoint and method of Phenomenology as such; only some of the more relevant and salient points will be referred to in this context. The said inadequacy of Phenomenology could, however, be traced to certain limitations of the former in its claim to be a full-fledged *transcendental* philosophy. (Here 'transcendental phenomenology' more than 'descriptive phenomenology', is in view.)

(a) Firstly, as *transcendental* enquiry, Phenomenology, it seems, does not succeed in exploring the ulterior nature and significance of pure consciousness, into the region of which it aims to investigate. The shortcoming in the 'essentialistic' search seems to be conspicuous in the final characterization—honest though it may be—of pure consciousness as "phenomenological residuum" (cf. Ideas α 33). But that looks more like an apologetic admission of a philosophical desideratum than an affirmation of the nature and status of consciousness. (b) The major philosophical inadequacy of Phenomenology in the strict sense seems to lie in its necessary confinement to the status of 'possibility' on the pathway of its analysis and even at the apex of its investigation. But it is dubitable if such 'possibility' devoid of reality-ground could stand further analysis. Consequently, the failure of pure phenomenology to yield the genuine *ontological* standpoint of Being—a question which is nevertheless involved in any serious phiolsophizing.

The absence in Husserl's Phenomenology of such a standpoint—ontological or metaphysical seems to have strengthened it as a rigorous presuppositionless science of philosophy (the aim of Husserl being to develop "philosophy as rigorous science")—but possibly at the cost of its further philosophical merit at large. In Advaita, on the other hand, the ontological standpoint is conspicuously present. So far as a pure metaphysic or critique of experience is concerned, the Advaitic doctrine of *Cit* is no doubt amenable broadly to phenomenological lines of analysis. But a genuine ontology being taken into consideration,—and Advaita is hardly to be understood apart from that—the phenomenological standpoint in itself may not evidently prove to be adequate.

How, then, is the alleged ontological standpoint to be obtained in the context of the Advaita doctrine of *Cit*—proceeding more or less in the path of transcendental analysis of experience? The present chapter and the next shall chiefly be concerned with this problem of finding a pathway to the metaphysics of Being, in line with the doctrine of *Cit* expounded so far. And here comes the question of out-stepping the bounds of *pure* phenomenology in favour of a supposedly more *concrete* approach.

It may at least here be remarked that Advaita, after all, would be the last philosophy to stop with *idealities*, which represent *ideal possibility* alone, and to refrain from positing Being as absolute *existence* (ontologically speaking). In this respect the notion of 'possibility' should prove particularly relevant, as defining the relation of the *ideal* and the *actual*. The position of Advaita in this context has accordingly to be considered.

* * *

The shortcoming of the purely phenomenological approach towards the Vedāntic metaphysic of experience may be evident, as the necessary *ontological* status of *Cit*—the supreme and ultimately the only essence—is taken into consideration. Thus, pure consciousness is not the mere transcendental presupposition, nor even the limiting point in phenomenological reduction. It is further posited as the prime existence-stratum, in terms of which reality is to be conceived on ultimate analysis. Thus for Vedānta, 'phenomenological residuum' would not be the final characterization of pure consciousness ; but it proposes to go beyond a metaphysically non-committal status. How that passage to the expressly positive standpoint of Being—a metaphysical standpoint *par excellence*—can be effected in the typically Vedāntic way, shall be shown in the next chapter.

* * *

A strictly phenomenological investigation would, as we have seen, hardly move beyond the region of pure *possibility* which is represented by the system of essences and wherefrom the ontic question of *existence* is sought to be shelved.* And the Advaitic principle of *Cit* has been worked out, in keeping with the phenomenological outlook, as *the* essence within the region of pure experience—its status being defined accordingly. Consequently, to be consistent with such phenomenological standpoint, the ontic status pertaining to *Cit* is ultimately to be defined purely in terms of *possibility*. [Our earlier investigations in Part I have also left *cit* with the tentative status of possibility – as *possible* autonomous subjectivity.]

However, it should be noted, genuine Advaita would not subscribe to an aprioristic approach as such—apriorities, either as pure concepts of thought or as pure essences, being not the concern of Advaita. It is rather with the question of *reality* that Advaita concerns itself. Nor would it be ready to bring down *cit*—in conformity with the phenomenological standpoint to the metaphysically undefined level of 'phenomenological residuum.' Yet, in reflectively approaching the ultimate principle of *Cit*, Advaita may primarily refer to the final and only essence of *possible* Reality, distinguished from the actual—such possibility being conveyed by reflective analysis itself.[1] But such an idea of possibility (*sambhāvanā-buddhi*) as born of reflection strengthens rather than dismisses the ontological ground posited by Advaita.

All that a purely phenomenological line of investigation may assure us is *cit* as the central essence behind all our experience, actual and possible—the essence, theoretically at least, being

*Cf. Husserl's general attitude that 'the knowledge of possibilities precedes the knowledge of actualities'.

divorced from existence. But the fundamental metaphysical interest of Advaita, on the other hand, lies in *existentiality* or in reality that exists *per se*. So the problem arises : how are we to reconcile these two apparently rival points of view in the understanding of Advaita, i.e., the phenomenological and the ontological ? The task is thus to find out whether and how an account in the light of possibility could yield at the same time existential reality.

Here, the *existentialistic* point of view may come in, proposing a *non-cognitive* approach to reality. But that would mean the abandonment of the cognitive approach so persistently followed by Advaita. So, the existentialistic approach can hardly be entertained, just because reflective analysis has to proceed in the pathway of *knowing*, whereby alone the question of possibility can arise. Thus, leaving aside the non-cognitive approach of the existentialist, the ontological possibility of the Advaitin should rather be considered in the light of knowing—and that may be characterized as *cognitive possibility*.

Apart from the different orientations of the concept of 'possibility' in different philosophies, metaphysical or non-metaphysical, let us consider what may broadly be regarded as the 'common-sense view,' and its further implications. As the common-sense view would state, every possible is real, unless it is contradicted. A content of experience brings with it a claim to reality or actual existence, but the negative condition of possible contradiction would be there. Consequently, whatever is presented as a *possible* content—and any content is a *possible* content—is to be taken as *primca facie* real so far as it is capable of standing possible contradiction. This position would be quite opposite to that of the positivist; for the latter, possibility itself is conceived in terms of reality or actual existence and not *vice versa* (as in Positivist thought). Such a notion of possibility should not be limited to the pragmatic standpoint of 'working abstraction' that owes its entire validity to actual experience alone. Also it need not be doubted that the distinction between actuality and possibility is altogether overlooked in such a view. For, to take the possible as equivalent to the real is not the same as to actualize or realize such reality; the latter would mean something more.

Again, to approach the question in a different way, the verdict of our common aesthetic experience also—as in the region of art and music—would hardly justify the status of such *bare* possibility as noted above. Thus, in the world of art, a masterpiece of painting such as an Ajanta fresco or the Mona Lisa of Da Vinci, for instance, would convey an ideal proportion or harmony of visible form. Or a song attuned to an Indian *rāga* would convey the ideal form of the *rāga* concerned. In neither case is the *ideal* form conceived through mere *abstraction* from the colours or the notes concerned; rather, in and through the latter the mind aesthetically feels the ideal (that is the *possible*) as concrete (and as realized), though in progressive steps. Thus the positivistic attempt to reduce ideality to a mere sensationalistic 'entropy', as it were, seems to be plainly going against the verdict of common aesthetic experience.

With the said common-sense interpretation, however, the Advaitic approach to the question of possibility would substantially agree. Thus for Advaita, every presentative content of experience —*viṣaya*—*prima facie* partakes of the status of the real but subject to the negative condition of cancellation (*bādha*). Any content may be taken as actually existent so far as it is not replaced by a new content at the self-same locus. The possible is thus envisaged *qua* real and not ideal abstraction or bare possibility.

The Advaitic theory of intrinsic validity of cognition—*Svataḥprāmāṇya*—conforms to this approach to the notion of possibility. According to *Svataḥprāmāṇya* theory the reality of the presented content makes itself felt at the very primary moment of cognition. With the Mīmāṃsakas, Advaita would hold that the object of cognition is real so far as cognition reveals it, and that a cognition is valid so far as it reveals some object. Consequently, cognition in revealing an object is necessarily valid. The intrinsic capacity of cognition for determining the object is recognised to be defining the very nature of epistemic validity (*prāmāṇya*) itself.[2] Thus the truth pertaining to the knowledge of object concerned is not to be regarded as an *added* property of the knowledge, gained through external corroborative or confirmatory processes of cognition and of practical test, as Nyāya would maintain.

A likely objection to the position of intrinsic validity of cognition would be : the question of validity could be of any meaning only in a reflective context where the 'truth-value' (as Hobhouse and others would term it) is involved. As left to itself at the primary moment, cognition should be free from any question of validity. But it may be replied, the actual existence of the object is communicated to us at the very primary moment of cognition. What a secondary cognition contributes is no *new* reality; there may only be a more *explicit* recognition of the self-same reality. There is no addition either with regard to the validity itself or to its apprehension.* As to the validity itself, the self-same truth present at the primary level reappears in a clearer form at the secondary; for, the reality of the object is present all the same at both the levels. As for the apprehension of the truth, whereas at the primary level the existence of the object in question is felt entirely in the object-context, the secondary confirmatory cognition pertains more specifically to the *existence* aspect of the object, more or less independent of the context of the content in view. The truth of the unreflective cognition is thus stated only in a new context in the reflective cognition, thereby gaining a new significance.

Also in examining the Nyāya position of extrinsic validity of knowledge—*parataḥ-prāmāṇya*—Advaita points out that testifying knowledge at the reflective level has no ontological bearing upon the existential truth already gained at the primary moment of cognition. For, subsequent associative and cohering cognition with regard to the object—the latter being involved only by way of reference not immediate—may have 'psychological' or 'aesthetic' value (to echo the logical positivist denunciation of metaphysics), which may be relevant to the knowing mind but not to the truth pertaining to the knowledge of object already gained. Viewed in this light, the standpoint of intrinsic validity need not basically come in conflict with the Naiyāyika contention as to extrinsic validity.

The question of *error* is worth mentioning in this connection, because the phenomenon of error may be pointed out as

***Vivaraṇa-prameya* refers to the question either of the origination (*utpatti*) or of the apprehension (*jñapti*) of the validity concerned, p. 100 f.

seemingly incompatible with the intrinsic validity of cognition. In its emphasis on the *presentative* basis of an erroneous cognition, Advaita would indeed agree with Nyāya as against the Prābhākara and the Bauddha. But in Nyāya theory of *Anyathākhyāti*, the belief in the *reality* of each possible seems to be overdrawn—(the appearing silver in the nacre is thus explained as *really* located in a different spatio-temporal situation). While Nyāya goes so far as to invest the content (*viṣaya*)at once with a reality-status, Advaita would not go further than ascribing on it a tentative and pragmatic (*vyāvahārika*) validity—a peculiar *neutral* status neither of reality nor of unreality—*sadasadvilakṣaṇatva* [see Ch. VI (5)]. As to the alleged cognition at the error stage, Advaita treats it not as knowledge proper but only as *seeming* knowledge (*jñānābhāsa*).*

The Advaitic interpretation of experience thus may be viewed as combining, in a way, two approaches to the concept of 'possibility' as could be found in modern Western philosophy—characterized respectively as the phenomenological and the metaphysical. The one, exemplified in the philosophy of Nicolai Hartmann, seems to result in a schism between the real and the ideal; the other, exemplified in the metaphysics of A. N. Whitehead, tends to posit *transcendent* entities by way of abstraction—though "eternal objects" and "actual occasions" in Whitehead are otherwise regarded as 'intrinsically inherent in the total metaphysical situation.' Coming back to the Vedāntic context, on the one hand, a broadly phenomenological mode of reflexion could possibly move towards the exploration of *Cit* as the central essence; on the other hand, *Cit* presents not merely the highest point of possibility in transcendental reflexion, but also claims absolute reality. *Cit* thus comes out as possibility qua reality.

Cit-essence, unlike Hartmannian 'Value', is not to be regarded as Platonic in its transcendentality. For it is, after all, obtained from within the region of 'purified' subjective experience in the wake of transcendental reflection, though it is not

* *Cf.* The distinction of nescience (*ajñāna*) in the aspect of object and of cognizance—the latter in terms of *ajñāna-vṛtti*. q. v. Ch. VI (6).

to be confined on ultimate consideration within such a sphere. *Cit* is sought to be traced in and through the phenomenal states of experience. At no stage of reflection—not even at the bodily level—is *cit* absent. At every stage *cit* is to be traced in varying association with the corresponding referential or functional correlate; the non-empirical fringe prevails behind the empirical mass. As Śaṅkara contends, consciousness is found to persist in and through all the three normal states of man—from waking to deep sleep.[3] With each stage of reflection, *cit* as the 'possible' comes out in greater purity of essence, progressively detached from the corresponding empirical implications. The import of 'thou' (*tvam*) in '*Tat tvam asi*' indicates the innermost self that comes out in stages of reflection right from the bodily level and ultimately proves to be the *possible* pure consciousness itself.[4]

Now, what precisely is meant by *cit* as conveying *possibility* ? Is it just an *ideal* demand of thought for the 'Ought-to-Be' ? That would indeed leave the possible without the reality-basis. But to refer back to the common-sense position, confirmed by Advaita, as already shown, every situation of 'possibility' involves also reality—subject to the absence of possible contradiction.

So viewed, the intermediate essences presented in the path of reflection should rather be interpreted as provisional possibles—such as may claim to be real prior to being contradicted by subsequent content of reflection. Such intermediate status is to be read as neither real nor unreal, *mutatis mutandis* neither completely possible nor completely non-possible—a status represented aptly by the Advaitic category of the inexplicable (*anirvācya*). Thus, whatever stands as possible is guaranteed reality—at least within the context of the relevant experience-continuum.

Following this line of approach, we would come to the *final* essence, the highest possibility. It is thus that *cit* is derived. *Cit* may be viewed exactly in the light of any other essence as revealed in the intermediate range of reflection. Thus on the one hand, it would present itself as *possible*, marked at the same time by *knowability*, at the terminal stage of transcendental reflection. On the other hand, it should be regarded as *real* so far as it is possible. However, the real crux of the problem on possibility would arise at the stage of ultimate essence. The highest of possibility should claim at the same time to be the highest of reality. *Cit* is the essence which not merely *demands** to be real as 'Ought-to-Be,' but which must *exist*—and exist ontologically.

The possible grounds for holding the existentiality of the supreme essence may be more closely considered.

(*a*) A unique peculiarity of the *cit*-essence proper—a peculiarity missing in preceding essences—has to be admitted. Intermediate essences come home to us only as themselves revealed by the central essence of *Cit* in the background. The varying modes of subjectivity present shades of essentiality only as reflecting the presuppositional consciousness, the ultimate revealing factor. However, so far as the ultimate essence of *cit* is concerned, it stands on a unique ground. It is, as we have formerly seen, essentially self-revealing (*svayaṃprakāśa*). From the point of view of evidencing at least, *cit* constitutes the ground of all other essence-forms within the region of consciousness. And so far as evidencingness constitutes the very essence of *cit*, what is foundational *ratio cognoscendi* proves to be so also *ratio essendi*.

(*b*) To refer to the theory of possibility as implied by Advaita each *possible* at the respective stage of transcendental analysis standsas real, subject to the absence of possible contradiction by subsequent content. Now, the *possible* as revealed at the terminal phase of transcendental analysis *ex hypothesi* would claim at least provisional reality. Here, however, the essence presents itself with the unique claim of absolute *uncontradictability* (*abādhitatva*). Advaita holds in broad the indestructibility of consciousness, the impossibility of its absolute negation (*atyantābhāva*). The possible absence of consciousness is inconceivable—in the sense that the chair, the table, this or that particular individual might possibly be conceived of as not being there in some point of time, past or future. There is indeed no theoretical limit to the possibility of non-existence in respect of any phenomenon that may

*We have freely used the expression 'demand'—borrowing the concept from Hartmann—for its suitability for the purpose of our discourse (particularly in this chapter).

come within the range of consciousness directly or indirectly. But the evidencing principle that stands behind every experience and every thought—even the suicidal thought of its own annihilation—can never be regarded as itself destructible. To recognise consciousness in its identical essence apart from varying modes of reference amounts to denying that it is temporally dentermind* in terms of origination and destruction.* As the author of *Pañcadaśi* urges, in a metaphorical vein but unambiguously: Consciousness, which neither arises nor sets, is self-shining.[7]

So what follows from the Advaitic position stated above is that *cit*, the ultimate essence of the subjective, does not just represent the limiting point of the knowable essence-possibilities in reflexion, but also reality *par excellence*. It is the essence which differs uniquely in status from any other essence. Its unfailing reality-claim may be viewed in the light of one phenomenon alone, viz., the 'I' that presents itself *indubitably*. The indubitability and peculiar immediacy of the subjective comes home to us primarily through the I-feeling. In *cit*, the same indubitability at the surface reappears in unconditoned freedom. The individual-bound *I* is tanscended in the pure essence of subjectivity—*deindividualized* as much as real. [Though *sākṣi-caitanya* marks the foundational essence within the range of individual consciousness, *cit* as existence *par excellence* is hardly to be confined within the bounds of the individual. Advaita ontology is ever directed to the trans-individual Existence.]

Thus the Advatic *Cit* stands for cognitive possibility *par excellence*—the highest Essence being shown to be as much *real* as *knowable*. Here, however, our next problem would arise. *Cit*, so far as it is *phenomenologically* interpreted in terms of essence, still stands as real *qua essence* but not *qua reality*. However, the supreme essence is also recognised to be unique

*Husserl's focus on transcendental consciousness as foundational bears an ontological overtone at certain places, and appears to ring almost a Vedântic note, when he speaks, for example, of "the immortality of the transcendental I" and of "the impossibility that the transcendental I were born". Further compare Husserl's observation : "Each human 'I' conceals in itself, in a certain way, its transcendental I, and the latter does not die nor does it originate; it is an eternal being in becoming."[6]

in status, as necessarily implying *existence*. And once such existentiality or reality of the essence is recognized, cognitive possibility also takes on a ne· significance. It no longer remains an ideal essence envisaged transcendental reflection, but demands concrete realization. Thus the problem of *actualizing* the possible as real comes in—a problem which has no less seriously been treated in Advaita philosophy.

1. Cf. "*Jñānānanda-sarvajñapratyagātmabhūtam brahma..niścāyayitum asamartha, api yuktayaḥ sadāvagate brahmaṇi sāmānyadvāreṇa sambhāvanābuddhihetavo bhavanti*" *Vivaraṇa*, V, p. 221.
2. "*Prāmāṇyam nāma jñānasya arthaparicchedasāmarthyam*", *Vivaraṇa-prameya-saṅgraha*, p. 101.
3. ... *caitanyasya tu suṣupte api anuvṛttim* .." S. B. B S., IV. i. 2,
4. Cf." . . . *tvampadārthopi pratyagātmā ... dehād ārabhya pratyagātmatayā sambhāvyamānaḥ caitanyaparyantatvena avadhāritaḥ*", idem.
5. Husserl, *Analyse zur passiven synthesis*, *Beilage* VIII, 10, Nijhoff,
6. ibid (my translation of the passage from the original German).
7. "*Nodeti nāstametyekā saṃvideṣā svayamprabhā*", *Pañcadaśī*, I. 7.

CHAPTER VIII

PASSAGE TO BEING : FAITH-APPROACH

It now appears that a purely transcendental-phenomenological standpoint, as exercised within the framework of Advaita Vedānta, could at least indicate pure consciousness to be a *real possibility* rather than a mere ideal presupposition. The ontological standpoint, on the other hand, proceeds to ensure the concrete reality-ground of such possibility; in other words, the possible turns to be the real—the highest of the possibles, thus, into the highest of the reals. In envisaging a transition from the one standpoint to the other—from the phenomenological to the ontological—a new step, which could overcome the necessary limitation of the purely reflective approach given so far, would be entailed. In this context there appears the role of faith—faith in scriptural authority or the verbal testimony of scriptures (*Śabda*).

Such scriptural faith has a twofold role to play in respect of gaining the final ontological standpoint in Advaita. At the first instance, it should bring home the positive assurance of the *knowability* of the sureme Essence *concrete*, i.e., as real or existent and not merely *qua* essence. Further, such assurance gained through verbal testimony should be carried to fulfilment in actual realization of Reality.

Faith—as we propose to characterize the Advaitic attitude in this context—though departing from the strictly rational and reflective approach, should not be taken as a mere non-cognitive attitude or a bare surrender of the cognitive. It does not stand for a premature emotive-volitional commitment by choosing to forgo progress of knowing—as Existentialists would generally do. It rather signifies a fulfilment of the *cognitive* demand itself, developed in the pathway of Advaita metaphysic of experience. It suggests a level which, though other than the intellectual, leads to the actualization of the demand for knowing Reality in concrete. Viewed in this light, scriptural faith should rather stand for an *enlightened irrationalism.* The possibility that the highest essence discovered in transcendental reflection, i.e., *cit* is at the same time real *per se,* is primarily given to us through a peculiar assurance resting upon the general Vedāntic tradition. Further, such assurance is ultimately carried to the stage of fullest comprehension of Reality or Being. For want of any other suitable expression, the whole province of this trans-rational approach may broadly be characterized as *Faith*— an approach grounded in Śruti.*

There are two implications of this faith-approach : (a) It refers to the tradition of scriptures (*Śruti*) as the repository of the highest spiritual truths and insights; (b) In a more ultimate sense, faith implies the *revelation* of Reality to the mind already enlightened through reflection. (In both cases, however, the reference is to *knowing.*) Accordingly follows the twofold treatment of the *alogism* involved in the final phase of the Advaitic metaphysic of experience.

A. The tradition of scriptural authority (*Śrutiprāmāṇya*) with regard to ultimate (metaphysical) truths has a significant bearing upon the Vedāntic discipline in its search for Reality. A statement contained in the scriptures (*āptavākya*) carries a special claim with the searching mind on the very strength of credibility born of tradition. As such it proves to be uniquely different in its truth-claim from any other ordinary statement. For the modern mind, however, to anchor a philosophical belief on mere traditional authority may seem to be the very antithesis of a genuinely philosophical endeavour. (The point is touched upon subsequently.)

---

*Even in the context of *religious* faith as generally interpreted in Western theology, the cognitive aspect as 'belief' may be distinguished from the volitional aspect as 'trust'—the former alone being relevant in theological discourse *cf.* "Faith", *Hastings' Encyclopedia of Religion and Ethics*, Vol. V. (1912), p. 689. (Of course, our discourse here proposes to be wholly *philosophical* and not theological.)

So, the Vedāntic appeal to verbal testimony of *Śruti* has to be viewed in the proper perspective. It is a truism that a philosopher has, after all, to participate in the concrete life-blood of his cultural tradition. Such tradition may have unique validity for the philosopher concerned—a validity which may normally be missed in tradition other than his own. So follows an *alogical* acceptance of the *reality* of such tradition even prior to a reflective and rational appreciation of its nature through distinguishment. Thus, when the philosopher accepts a tradition—granting it to be a living one—the attitude that is involved may be characterized as *existentialistic,* in a broad sense of the term. It is a primary existentialistic faith in the authority of *Śruti* that imparts special significance to scriptual statements.

Such metaphysical assurance, derived from verbal testimony, may well be explained with reference to ordinary verbal cognition in the empirical sphere. Thus, while any spoken word conveys nothing more than *bare* possibility as regards the actual existence of the meant or referrent of the word, such *prima facie* belief would vary according to the hearer's faith in the speaker concerned—the presence of what Stebbing calls "the hearer-speaker attitude" being taken for granted. When a fact is stated by one in whom I have faith (in the ordinary sense of reliability), I tend to believe the fact to be an actuality even though it be beyond the range of my experience at the moment. The case would, however, be different when I have scarcely any faith in the person stating or the speaker.

However, verbal faith derived from *ordinary* speech would evidently fall short of the faith derived from the verbal testimony of scriptures at least in two important respects —even when the element of primary faith in the speaker be granted in common in both the cases. Firstly, unlike ordinary speech, scriptural testimony does not offer any possibility of empirical verification, the truth-content here being ex-hypothesi *non-empirical.* Secondly, what is conveyed by ordinary speech is, after all, *bare* possibility which in all case falls short of concrete possibility. The verbal testimony of *Śruti,* on the other hand,—usually represented by the preceptor (*guru*) in whom the student hearing is supposed to have full faith (*śraddhā*)—necessarily yields complete *valid* possibility. Such verbal testimony guarantees the *reality* of the supreme essence of reflection independent of the context of the latter, and also the ultimate comprehension of Reality *in concrete.*

It is, however, to be noted that even the verbal testimony of scriptures can *prima facie* yield only mediate (*parokṣa*) and not immediate knowledge. Nevertheless, the mediate knowledge as to the nature and existence of Being, so produced through the verbal source, enjoys validity on its own account—thanks to the scriptural source itself. And this is what distinguishes such knowledge from the mediate knowledge derived from common inference (*anumāna*). Inference as an independent way of knowing fails as such to lead to *ontological* possibility, which however can be communicated by the scriptural statements. In the field of empirical knowledge, inference may provide some sort of possibility (in the form of verifiability), though on the basis of available data. In verbal cognition from *Śruti* where the transcendent non-empirical reality is meant, there is hardly any scope for empirical verification. What is missing in (empirical) verification is, however, more than gained on ground of verbal testimony, which itself claims to embody experience at the highest level.

This approach through faith in the form of verbal testimony may be clearer if we cite by contrast the major approaches to *cognitive faith* which may be cited in European thought. Thus comes into view the approach of *pure thought* ('Transcendental reflection') as may be found (a) *positively,* in the Rationalist system of the continent and (b) *negatively,* in Kantianism.

(a) The Rationalist belief, shared by a host of thinkers from Descartes to Wulf and Leibniz, assumes that pure *a priori* thinking gives us valid cognitive possibility regarding transcendent metaphysical truths. And the world-views they respectively present are but the elaborations of pure categories of transcendental thought in its *a priori* movement. Now such categories are posed as pure *universals,* distinguished reflectively. But the very possibility of *absolutely* dissociating universals of pure reason from particulars of experience may be put to question. For the honest verdict of thought seems to be that pure universals, as completely dissociated from particulars, should rather stand as *ideal* 'demands' than as *real* categories.

(b) It is from this negative criticism of the rationalist position that Kantianism takes its origin. Kant, proceeding through transcendental reflection to *a priori* modes of thinking, comes to a negative position so far as the ontological possibility of the *a-priorities* of thought is concerned. The movement of transcendental thought by way of distinguishment seems with Kant to reach its apex in 'Transcendental Ideas'; the latter, though the highest target of thought, miss philosophical validity in neither bearing upon actual experience nor possessing existence by themselves. Kant, not ready to sacrifice cognitive possibility, prescribes a veritable stage-back to the level of actuality of sense-experience. Reality is to be sought nowhere else than on the sense-level. Highest universals or pure concepts may arise as mere *demands* of pure reason with no possibility of their actualization as real. The path of transcendental reflection, remains. after all, to be linked to the actuality of sense experience. (However, Kant's concern for metaphysical reality made its way through the path of "practical reason".)

This Kantian critique of pure thought in the face of the rationalist doctrine may find its echo in the Advaitic treatment of *universal* (*sāmānya*) in opposition to the Naiyāyika view. Advaita, though tentatively admitting universals in its reflective enquiry, would stop short of positing *metaphysical* universals, existing *per se* and completely dissociated from the particulars. The ideality of universals is to be recognized, but in and through the system of particulars and not exclusively beyond that. This is where Advaita would sharply differ from the Nyāya-Vaiśeṣika standpoint which would too boldly posit *metaphysical* universals—standing on that account on the same platform as the Greek masters, Plato and Aristotle. Of course, Advaita seems *prima facie* to admit of at least two universals, viz., *Cit* and *Sat* (Existence). Yet, even such universals would hold good rather as transcendental categories in the path of reflection, and could further be posited as metaphysically real on the strength of scriptural faith alone. At the final stage of concrete realization, the two evident universals would prove to be but

Reality itself or Being that is the concrete embodiment of *Cit* and *Sat* at the same time.

B. The Advaitic search after Reality would not stop with the assurance of *realizability* born of verbal testimony. It passes on to the final phase of realization itself—to the complete actualization of the *possibility* as pertaining to the supreme essence. The reflective grasp of supreme essence through transcendental analysis, supported by scriptural authority, is ultimately to mature into the concrete immediacy of Reality. Here the typical issue of knowledge from verbal testimony—*śabdajanya-jñāna*—would come into play.

Such cardinal scriptural text as 'Thou art that' (*Tattvam asi*) has a direct bearing upon the Vedāntic discipline, not as merely theoretical statements but as the point of departure for enlightenment through integral comrehension of Reality. The latter alone marks the final aim of Vedānta. The primary knowledge of Reality, with all the certainty as may be derived from scriptural texts, does not by itself imply the fullest comprehension. Scriptural texts are not, for the matter of that, without any efficacy for bringing about final enlightenment. In common experience we do find words serving as useful agents for bringing home direct to the wandering mind the truth it has been searching without success. The analogy of 'the tenth man' (*Daśamastvamasi*)—a homely example in Advaita literature—strikes on this very point.* In this case, a *demonstration* occurs within a context that gives significance to the object (or person) demonstrated. In the ideal stage of perfect realization of identity between "that" and "thou", however, the common distinction between the "descriptive" and the "demonstrative" uses of language (*cf.* Stebbing)[1] would not hold good—both "thou" and "that" being referred to as much *demonstratively* as *descriptively*.

---

*In *Bhāmatī*, I. i. l, another example is given on a similar point. For a musical trainee, who is trying to grasp the exact note occurring in a certain *rāga*, a statement of the relevant note (or notes) may help his discriminating the note in actual perception. (It is thus that the science of music actually comes to facilitate the practical learner of music.)

Cognition through word (*śabda*) is to be analysed further in steps of Vedāntic realization. Firstly, there arises from scriptural texts an *indirect* knowledge concerning the *existence* of Supreme Being. There are texts declaring the latter as *real* (*sat*), as *existing* (*asti*). All that such existential statements yield is the assured but still *indirect* knowledge of Reality. In its lack of directness, it is no less mediate (*parokṣa*) than inferential cognition, as already pointed out. It is only the generic aspect of existentiality (*sattvāṃśa*) that is *primarily* conveyed through scriptural texts, as also from ordinary words or inference; but the *specific* content (*vyakti*) is not revealed thereby. To state the situation in a different way, viz.. in terms of *ajñāna*—the ignorance in respect of existence would be removed while one may still be in the dark as to the actual manifestation of the meant content—*abhānāpādaka-ajñāna*).[2]

In order that the instruction in scriptural texts may yield its intended result, viz., the fullest comprehension of Self, the import of the texts concerned implying Reality must be understood.[3] The intermediate stages of gradual apprehension of the ultimate essence, finally meant by the texts, are thus necessitated. Steps of knowledge, in the understanding of the true essence of Self as distinguished from its inessential aspects, are presupposed.[4] Through repeated guidance from relevant scriptural texts, the gradual grasp of *the* Essence is effected in progressive approximation. Thus, as on the one hand inessential implicate are dissociated, so on the other the underlying essence-contens would present itself as more and more purified. For the ultimate essence, i.e., the essence that stands behind all intermediate essences, remains involved within the manifold associations of body, sense-organs, mental factors and so on.

So far as the steps of reflection are prompted by scriptural instructions, the immediacy of knowledge resulting from scriptural statements, even if admitted, should hardly be taken without qualification. Indeed the *Bhāmatī* school of Advaita stresses the *mediacy* of knowledge as effected through verbal testimony—*śābdaparokṣavāda*—rather than its *immediacy*—*śābdāparokṣa*—as the *Vivaraṇa* school would prefer to hold. Along with the advocated immediacy of knowledge necessarily goes the *Vivaraṇa* insistence on the *injunctive* approach—an injunction of law (*niyama-*

vidhi)in respect of knowledge of Reality. Such injunction should not, however, conflict with the thoroughly *cognitive* attitude of Advaita, if we consider the distinction between the initial phase of enquiry (*jijñāsā*) and the final phase of knowledge amounting to the perfect comprehension of Self that is Reality on the last analysis.

The position of Vācaspati Miśra, advocating the mediacy of knowledge born of verbal testimony, is apparently opposed to the *Vivaraṇa* view. But in exaggerating the external difference, the essential agreement bearing upon the fundamentally *cognitive* approach is apt to be overlooked.* The *Vivaraṇa* school, while advocating the immediate character of scriptual knowledge, maintains at the same time that subsequent reflection and meditation are necessary to yield immediate revelation of Reality. The purification of the mind is insisted upon. As Śaṅkara remarks, the realization of Self may be attained by the mind, purified through proper discipline and aided by scriptural instructions from the teacher (who should enjoy the fullest reliance of the student).[5]

The real point behind the controversy is : what comes to us primarily as a *bare* possibility is to mature, through steps of mental discipline and reflection, into *valid* possibility, and ultimately into the very concrete immediacy of the Real itself. According to Śaṅkara himself, for the ordinary individual not yet endowed with an intellectual understanding of the Real, there is certainly the necessity of repeated scriptural instruction (*śravaṇa*) and reflection, intellectual and transcendental—*manana* and *nididhyāsana*.† For those also, who have already attained clear and distinct insight into the two principles of Being (*Tat*) and of the individual self (*tvam*), the efficacy of scriptural statements in producing the immediater revelation of the Real in absolute Identity is no less there.[6]

**Cf.* Pointing to the fundamental agreement between the two views, Dr. Mahadevan thus remarks : "...both Vācaspati and the Vivaraṇakāra agree in this that the path to perfection lies in and through knowledge", T. M. P. Mahadevan, *The Philosophy of Advaita*, p. 254.

†*Manana* and *nididhyāsana* need not be taken as two exclusive stages, signifying intellection and meditation respectively, but may better be taken as respectively less and more intense stages of the continuous movement of 'transcendental reflection'. Vide *supra*, Ch. V (2).

In this context, the notion of 'demand' (already introduced in our discourse in the last chapter) may be found particularly relevant. As the ultimate essence is recognised—though not immediately but distantly—to be *real*, the demand for actualizing it in existence arises. The elaboration of the nature of reality clarifies the demand, while the progressive approximation of the essence of consciousness in steps of transcendental reflection strengthens it. So far as the fulfilment of the final demand is concerned, it is to be gained, if at all, at a level beyond the region of transcendental reflection—a level where Being is to prevail absolutely by itself.

The said *demand* as brought out in the wake of transcendental reflection may well be confirmed by the fundamental *value*-attitude, basically characterizing the outlook of Advaita philosophy. The *interest* in reality is essentially an attitude of value, seeking satisfaction in nothing short of concrete existence. The Advaitin would share the common interest of Indian philosophy—and quite pronouncedly too—in Freedom (*mokṣa*) as the supreme end (*parama-puruṣārtha*). [Indeed *Freedom*, for Advaita, is the very Reality itself, eternally accomplished (*pariniṣṭhita*) in nature.] The value-attitude being present at the root, the interest in reality necessarily preponderates over a merely *theoretical* enquiry into a system of *possible* categories. As the ultimate essence of transcendental reflection represents supreme value too, the former is promoted, by virtue of value-demand, to the highest existence-stratum. Nothing short of concrete reality could satisfy the Advaitin; he would not merely stop with the realization of Reality as 'Ought-to-Be'. This Advaitic attitude may in one sense appear to be somewhat Kierkegaardian, in its interest in the existential question, in concrete existence—an attitude that marks itself as different from the disinterestedness in respect of the possible.*

*There may be an interesting study on the equation of existence and value in Indian thought. In the concept of existentiality (*sattā*) there is the implication of *value*, the highest of existence or reality thus implying value *par excellence*. That which is the highest good (*śreya*) must be existent. Value without the existential bas is would be futile.

Further significance of this resulting phase of the Advaitic metaphysic of experience may be brought out in the light of a *metaphysical* interpretation. What demands finally to be realized should evidently be *trans-individual*, for the real that is supposed to exist absolutely *per se* must be so beyond the context of individual consciousness. As such, it may be spoken of indefinitely as the Supreme Being. Now, the unqualified ontological status of the said Supreme Being may also be viewed from a different angle in the light of the so-called 'revelation' on the part of Being to the mind in reflection. What the mind grasps in clear understanding as the ultimate Being that *demands* to be real but falls short of being realized in perfect immediacy, would find its transcendent counterpart in *revelation* on the part of Being itself.*

Further, such metaphysical revelation or the immediacy of absolute trans-individual reality might even be indicated at certain cardinal stages in the path of transcendental reflection. Such stages of revelation, however, need not be regarded as strictly conforming to the Vedāntic system as it stands. By way of freely interpreting the Advaitic metaphysic of experience alone do we prefer to introduce the concept of revelation here. Thus right from the level of gross body (*sthūla-śarīra*) upwards, the outstanding phases of essence-structure, obtained through upward steps of intuition, could possibly be correlated to the progressive revelation of (trans-individual) reality as *cosmic*. [The cosmic principles of *Hiraṇyagarbha* and *Virāṭ*, mentioned in the earlier Vedāntic literature, may be looked upon as such projected categories which constitute the possible ontologic-cosmological scheme of Advaita, developed in the line of its metaphysic of experience.]

---

*'Revelation' in this context is to be understood independent of any necessary religion-theological association of divine personality as such. Here the expression indicates the transferred perspective of Being—vis-a-vis the human mind envisaging Being in reflection—in its total immediacy and identity. Looked at in this perspective, the idea of ontological revelation could possibly come close to the exposition of the question of Being by later Heidegger, with his accent on the "revelatory essence" of Being. The "illumination of Being", according to Heidegger, lies in its essential "unconcealedness".

In this connection, it may not be out of place to hint at a further possible 'religious' significance following from such metaphysical notion of revelation. What has been explained as *demand* could also possibly be connected to the idea of 'grace', variously occurring in different theistic philosophies of India and the West. With the recognition of *personality* in the reality-principle, the line of communication between the human mind and the Divine seems itself to take on a *human* colour. Thus, what stands as the revelation of Being to the enquiring mind, when viewed in the *Bhakti* perspective, for instance, may also prove to be the 'grace of God' upon the devotee concerned. Leaving aside theology as such and keeping more to phenomenology, the demand of the aspiring and reflecting individual (*jiva*) seems to correspond to the notion of 'grace' of the Divine Being.

From such an interpretation of Advaitic enlightenment in terms of the so-called *revelation*, one seeming difficulty may however arise. The very conception of the accomplished Reality revealing itself to the reflecting subject seems to imply a total departure from the subjectivity-oriented direction pursued so far. For is it not true that the concept of revelation carries with it the usual implication of *objective* reality as standing in opposition to the subject ? This objection can be met in the present context if we bear in view that here revelation is to be understood as the very realization of subjectivity itself. And subjectivity realized is objectivity denied.

In cases other than pure *cit*, the revealed content would stand relatively independent even while the context of subjective evidencing were there. From the objects of sense-perception to the essences of transcendental reflection, there would hardly be any exception to this presentative character. But with regard to *cit*, the central essence of subjectivity, it would be otherwise. For, to speak of *cit* as finally *revealed* should not mean its being presented to the reflecting subject—as *other* than the latter. As on the one hand, revelation (*prakāśa*) constitutes the essential nature of *cit* as self-evidencing, the latter in its turn constitutes the very essence of the subject itself—a point made in our earlier chapters.

Yet, a revelatory presentative character may not altogether be ignored in the final comprehension of *cit* as real. But such revelatory character too would prove to be but self-transcending on ultimate analysis; for even the context of *approach* on the part of the reflecting mind would be missing, as revelation were finally to culminate in Being itself. Of course, Being can not be regarded as *subjective*, because subjectivity, after all, would refer to the context of the intuiting consciousness. Nor can it be regarded as object.* But knowing and being—subjectivity and object-hood—appear ultimately to be transcended in the common ground of Reality, which could be characterized to be as much subjective as objective—or rather beyond the subject-object frame of reference altogether.†

Now, to come back to the analysis of knowledge through verbal testimony, it is admitted by the Advaitin that the final immediacy of the Real is gained through knowledge born of scriptural statement. The final stroke of illumination works its way through the *integral* mode of consciousness—*akhaṇḍadhī*—having for its content the self-accomplished Being itself. In such knowledge alone could Reality in its concreteness—so far reflectively envisaged as Essence—stand comprehended. Such final and fullest comprehension is meant by the Advaitic stress on *knowledge* as the pathway to Reality.

Nevertheless, it may be argued that even the ultimate mode (*vṛtti*) should not be free from at least the last vestige of Nescience (*avidyā*). The final mode, however, would bear a peculiarly *transitional* character—and a transition towards the Real. Consciousness as reflected in the final mode seems to be 'overwhelmed', as it were, by the Real itself, its alleged content. The highest point in the distinguishment of essence would at the same time mark unreserved *identification*—as the essence can

*Some later Advaitins—such as the authors of *Vedānta-paribhāṣā*, *Advaita-siddhi* etc. represent the Vedāntic Absolute more in the light of the grand metaphysical 'Object'. But the characterization of Being simply *objectwise* seems to ignore completely the subjective approach which is so vital in grasping *Cit* as supreme Essence. The final acceptance of reality or ontological existence need not overlook the pathway leading to the pen-ultimate stage.

†*Cf.* It is thus that the Upaniṣadic dictum "*Brahmavid brahmaiva bhava*", closely bearing upon Advaita philosophy, may be understood.

no longer be grasped as a content presented to detached evidencing. The purest essence, so far intuited in progressive approximation, emerges as Reality, engulfing in unconditioned identity both the evidenced and the evidencing—the two only *seemingly* distinguished. The immediacy of the integral mode of consciousness (which can hardly be regarded as a 'mode of consciousness' proper) still pertaining to *jīva*, would directly pass on to the Real, as it were.* From the ontological standpoint, the immediacy originally belongs to the real indeed; but from the point of view of transcendental reflection i.e., *ratio cognoscendi*, the immediacy would primarily pertain to the knowledge concerned. However, the final emphasis of Advaita is on the *ontological* standpoint of Existence. Such final transition into the Real hardly admits of any further analysis and would rather call for an *existential* mode of understanding. Thus at the apex of reflective distinguishment, Existence reigns supreme in non-distinguishment.

To proceed further with the significance of existentiality thus attained through the integral mode of knowing, it brings with it a new *context* beyond that of the intuiting consciousness—the latter persisting, however thinly, in the final knowledge. The ultimate essence of the subjective reveals itself not in the context of the subject but as transcending into the trans-subjective Real. Thus, what is metaphysically referred to as 'That' (*tat*) meets on common ground of transcendental reflection the essential subjectivity pertaining to individual consciousness (*tvam*). It is like re-discovering one's being in a new context—as the 'tenth man' realises himself as the tenth, this tenth-character really belonging to him though hidden from his notice. The character of the new metaphysical context of Being alone (*sadeva*) was known in the form of 'that'. [The very pronoun 'that' (*tat*), standing for the Real in question, implies some sort of *distance*—a distance for the enquiring consciousness.] But the realization of the said context—not qua *context* but qua *existence in concrete*—is sought to be effected through verbal

*Cf. *Pañcadaśī*, VII. 49-50. The author, in keeping with the general trend of Advaita Vedānta, refers to the two types of immediacy (*aparokṣatva*) —one pertaining to the final mode of consciousness (*akhaṇḍākāra-vṛtti*) and the other to the *object* corresponding to such mode, i.e., the self-manifest reality—the immediacy of the former being actually derived from that of the latter.

testimony concerning the supreme identity.*

From the foregoing treatment of the Advaitic transition from the strict bounds of a metaphysic of experience to an ontological standpoint of Existence, we are now in a position to assess the *existentialistic* step involved therein. The grounds for regarding the resulting position of Advaita as *existentialistic* —of course, in a wider sense—may be considered as follows.

(a) *Cit* as the highest essence, transcendentally derived, is recognised to be existentially real. It is not a question of positing existence as a *concept* at the height of possibility and of relating it externally to the highest essence of subjectivity. Rather, *cit* itself is *concretely* realized as existence. The Advaitin, like the true existentialist, would not be concerned with existence as a conceptual essence distinguished in abstraction but should rather be interested in concrete existence.† The ontological interest in the real throughout marks the transcendental enquiry

---

*Ultimate Reality—*Brahman* of Advaita Vedānta (originally of the Upaniṣads) conceived as absolutely transcendent, beyond all possible reference of consciousness, appears to be the ultimate *demand* of the philosophic consciousness. Advaita Vedānta, in its metaphysical thrust, moves on to the radical end of not resting with such a 'demand' qua 'demand', but of positing it as eternally realized in Brahman. Proceeding as we do in the path of a metaphysic of experience, Advaita could as well be represented as terminating in the Supreme Being (*Parameśvara*), standing as non-different in essence from the 'transcendental subject' (which would otherwise be the 'free self') in a unique relation of identification (*sāyujya*). Śaṅkara does sometimes use *Parameśvara* and *Brahman* as mutually interchangeable synonymous expressions. On a free interpretation, *Parameśvara* could be translated in terms of the highest possible phase of transcendental experience, and Brahman as the highest metaphysical demand even beyond the stage of *Parameśvara*. Hence the only language in respect of such Absolute, the ultiamate Transcendent, could be nothing other than that of the 'Indeterminate' and 'Ineffable' (*nirviśeṣa*, *nirguṇa* etc.)—all of which appear to be close enough to the Mādhyamika Absolute as Śūnya (i.e., *catuṣkoṭivinirmukta*).

†There is also a trend, as mentioned earlier, in later Advaita towards an independent metaphysics of Sat, proposing rather a conceptualistic approach to the question of Being. But even there the crux should remain as to how to effect the change-over from the *essence* of Existence to *real* existence. For even with the discovery of 'Existence' as the *central* essence, the real as existent may still remain unaccomplished. Thus the question of existentiality may be raised and to meet it some kind of *existentialistic* step seems to be entailed. *cf.* Kant's criticism on the 'Ontological Argument' Vide. *supra.* Introduction.

of Advaita. And it is nowhere so evident as in the question of final comprehension, which again is marked by the priority of existence over essence.

(b) The existentialistic import comes out further in the *non-intellectual* approach of faith as implied by the significant role attached to verbal testimony (*śabda*). Faith in *śabda* involves in two-fold steps a *non-cognitive* assurance of the existent real. The assurance first comes in the form of valid possibility yielded by *śabda*; and it is realized in perfect comprehension. Faith thus marks the point of departure in the quest for Reality.

(c) Moreover, the attitude of *value* is markedly present in Advaita in its supreme interest in ultimate freedom (*mokṣa*). And it is this basic value-attitude that makes for the ontological interest in concrete reality. To echo S. Kierkegaard, the value-interest (Kierkegaard speaks of 'the ethical') refuses to stop with 'the disinterestedness of the possible' in its interest for existence and for nothing short of existence.

However, even viewed in the light of an existentialistic attitude, the Advaitic position should be sharply distinguished from the strictly existentialist position as presented in recent European movement—from Kierkegaard to Sartre and Marcel etc. In the first place, the emotive-volitional approach as characterizing the irrationalism of the existentialist would sharply differ from what may be considered the *enlightened irrationalism* of Advaita. Whatever irrationalism may be involved in Advaita by way of faith seems to be directed to the interest of a higher level of knowing. Though *śabda* implies faith that is existential, it provides but the inevitable step to that final enlightenment into which transcendental reflection is to culminate.* Yet it may broadly be contended that the

---

*Such a stage of the highest possible experience may perhaps legitimately be characterized as 'mystical'—a completely supra-intellectual stage of 'higher immediacy' (Bradley), However, our concern is with the (cognitive) approach in the light of which even such ultimate mysticism, if at all, may be assessed.

N.B.—The Christian existentialist, Marcel speaks of 'revelation' in the sense of 'certain higher modes af human experience' through which 'the ontological mystery' may be comprehended. (*Vide* Gabriel Marcel, *The Philosophy of Existence*).

Advaitic metaphysics of the Real is in the long run effected on the fulcrum of existential faith.

Yet the principal distinction in character and thrust between Advaitic metaphysics and Existentialist ontology could hardly be overlooked. For the thoroughgoing existentialist, with his commitment of existentiality at the primary level of human reality, there would be virtually no transcendence beyond the bounds of the latter to a trans-personal ontological ground of existence. Although the 'Question of Being' (*Seinsfrage*) has conspicuously been put forward by Heidegger in his later phase, the task of rejoining Being, otherwise indefinable, to the human situation is never claimed to have been completed. If the essentialist foreshortens the question of Being, Heidegger finds the Being in question still existentially unabridged. However, in his total accent on a universal ontology ("fundamental-ontology") rather than on a philosophical theory of man, Heidegger's complete shift to the ontological standpoint of Being shows itself. Thus the search for the essence of man gives way to the question of Being—the humanity of man posed entirely from the point of view of "the proximity of Being".*

All this looks strangely similar to the Advaitic position, where also the ontological standpoint of Being, that is, *Ātman* or *Brahman*, prevails in the exposition of the nature of human existence. In Vedānta, however, the quest for Being (*Brahma-jijñāsā*) is not quite identical with the Heideggerian 'Question of Being'—the background of what Heidegger calls "European nihilism" being explicitly taken into account in the latter.† Being in Vedānta is rather the ever-present element of Reality in which man lives, moves and has his being, and also strives to find his way back to the Source.

Again, the rock-bottom tradition of scriptural statements—call it faith (cognitive faith)—conveys to the authentic

---

*As Heidegger characteristically declares, "Man is in the service of Being; he is the shepherd. not the lord."

†How far Śaṅkara could have been prompted by way of a reaction to the 'nihilistic' overtone (to say the least) of Mādhyamika Absolutism (*Śūnyavāda*) may, however, be left in the present discourse an open question. Accordingly, a closer parallel between Heidegger and Śaṅkara might possibly be worked out to that extent.

student of Vedānta the deep assurance of actualizing the highest ontological possibility of undifferenced unity (*advaita*). The final state of uttermost oneness could, of course, be pronounced as 'mystical'; but the issue of cognitive possibility of Being, emerging from a reflective analysis of experience, with its structure of constitutive essences, certainly brings into focus a philosophical concern.

The unique integration of the elements of immanence and transcendence, combining the immanentist explorations of the region of consciousness with the absolutely indeterminate Transcendent ('beyond the grasp of language and mental comprehension'—*avākmānasagocara*), the paradoxical meeting of the positive transparency of the evidence of consciousness with the utter ineffability of Being—that is the challenging synthesis Advaita presents. Instead of sharpening its tools on the edges of paradoxes—which could be one way of treating the whole situation of ineffability—Advaita would prefer the way of exploring the network of human experience in depth, by way of withdrawal and dissociation in reflexion, through the guidance of insights derived from faith. For the Advaitin, this is far from being an unholy marriage of understanding and faith; on the contrary, that implies for him the only sensible and worthwhile mode of thinking activity.

Similarly also, the value attitude, so markedly present in Advaita, has to find its root deeper than what might just be called the 'ethical' (as Kant or Kierkegaard, for example, would have it). It may, after all, be questioned as to how far the said 'ethical' could truly represent the total 'metaphysical demand' of human nature, as urged by Kierkegaard himself. The Advaitic value-demand, it is evident, cannot be fulfilled on the level of action or prescription, but rather on the level of truth, where the pathway of knowledge (*jñāna*) consummates.

Thus the ontological focus of Advaita is fixed on Being, and its metaphyiscs derived accordingly. The accent is not on the individual being qua individual but qua the trans-individual Being. The total metaphysical outlook of Advaita can accordingly be summed up, after Śaṅkara himself, as follows: Understanding the Supreme Being (*Parameśvara*) as Self (*ātmā-*

ityeva) would not mean the mundaneity of the former; what is intended, on the other hand, is to show that the world-involved being (*jiva*), in his ultimate essence, is grounded in the Supreme Being, rather than resting in his natural worldliness.[7] Here lies the perpetual challenge of human self-transcendence, the ever-present horizon of man's self-understanding.*

NOTES AND REFERENCES

1. Stebbing. *A Modern Introduction to Logic.* Ch. II. 2.
2. Cf. *Pañcadaśī*, VII. 56.
3. *Cf.* "*Padārtha-jñānapūrvakatvāt vākyārtha-jñānasya*", S. B. B. S., IV. i, 2; also, "*Vākyārthapratītiḥ sākṣātkārasya pūrvarūpam*", *Bhāmatī*, IV. i. 3.
4. ". . .*kramavatī pratipattiḥ tat tu pūrvarūpameva ātmapratipatteḥ* . . .", S.B.B. S., loc. cit.
5. "*Śāstrācāryopadeśa-śamadamādisaṃskṛtam mana ātmadarśane kāraṇam*", S. B. *Bhagavadgītā, II.* 21.
6. S. B. B. S., IV· i. 3.
7. ". . *saṃsāriṇaḥ saṃsāritvāpohena īśvarātmatvam pratipādayiṣitam*", S. B. B. S., IV. i. 3.

*Here, again, the use of the expression "*Parameśvara*"—rather than *Brahman*—though apparently bearing a theistic overtone, need not be viewed in any way as a departure from the basic critique of human subjectivity as Advaita provides it (see footnote on p. 122). Besides, the accent of the Sūtra concerned ("*Ātmā iti tūpagachhati grāhayanti ca*"), as commented upon by Śaṅkara, is, of course, the theme of Identity.

EPILOGUE

The search for a standpoint in respect of Advaitism—one that may legitimately yield a possible system of analysis of experience—brought us originally to the notion of subjectivity. Epistemologically speaking, it appears to be a philosophy wedded to the standpoint of subjectivity—or rather, transcendental subjectivity. But subjectivism is never the last word in Advaita; for metaphysically, it is attuned to Being, Being that is Consciousness. So far as a system of critique of experience goes, Advaita seems to hold alliance with Phenomenology in suggesting pure consciousness as the ground for all meanings of objectivity. As a full-fledged ontology of Being, on the other hand, there seems to be in a sense some kinship with existentialist thought, so far as the prime existential-reality of *Cit* as the highest precondition of knowledge and experience is at the same time stressed.

Now, a transcendental analysis of experience, it is true, would save Advaitism from turning its basically experientially-oriented philosophy into a dogmatic and barren metaphysics. However, such an analysis need not, on the other hand, take the shape of a purely theoretic system of idealities, oriented entirely in epistemological-methodological terms—as it tends to be in Husserlian phenomenology, which is proposed as a rigorous science of essences. For, with Vedānta, its characteristic hold on Being in concrete would hardly make way for a theoretic philosophy concerned solely with the elucidation of the 'meaning of being' (*Seinssinn*, according to Husserl). What pure phenomenology chooses to forgo in the interest of theoretic reflexion—leaving aside, however, the question of *reflexion* itself involving philosophical 'praxis' as recognised by later Husserl—is the commitment to reality in the form of naive world-belief; and that seems hardly to be regained on the ontological plane. Although transcendental subjectivity is posited as constituting, in the last analysis, world-meaning, it is never properly granted an ontological status in phenomenological philosophy itself.* Nor would consciousness, in a strictly phenomenological frame of reference, be existentially affirmed. Thus pure consciousness, though definitely indicated as the uniquely inner dimension, other than the 'natural', still remains, after all, the presupposed platform for methodological reflexion. The Advaitic thrust is certainly not confined within such methodological frame of reference.

Now in the Advaita system the existential affirmation of the reality of pure consciousness has been accomplished in two major steps. Negatively, there is a departure from a purely theoretic objective—the latter being marked by an interest in idealities or essence-forms, which have necessary bearing on the *meaning* of being rather than its reality. This finds its echo, on the positive side, in the pronounced affirmation of metaphysical faith in scriptural testimony assuring the ultimate ontological ground of transcendental subjectivity.

The transition into the said ontological ground could, of course, be effected through a fundamental recognition of the ulterior human end (*puruṣārtha*) and of corresponding disvalue (*anartha*), integrated to insights into the basic structure of experience. For in positing self as existence of a unique sort and seeking to realize it in its non-objective primordial existentiality, Advaitism no doubt puts forward a deep-lying value-concern, which determines and permeates the direction as well as the consummation of its total metaphysical endeavour. The issue of existence thus no longer remains a separate one. Besides the drive to *jijñāsā* towards *mokṣa*, there is also a direct cognizance of the value aspect of self. Such accent on self as value may well be traced in the cryptic Vedāntic formulation regarding *Ātman* : *asti bhati priyam*—that which exists, manifests and is at the same time most cherished. (The last aspect of '*priyam*' corresponds to the element of *Ānanda* in the composite statement of the Absolute as *Sat-Cit-Ānanda*†.

*Husserl in his later phase seems, however, to tend towards a metaphysical position, though not formulated in definite terms, in the trail of his conception of the 'world-constituting subjectivity'. Cf. *The Crisis European Science and Transcendental Phenomenology* and *Cartesian Meditations*.

†This direction in the characterization of *Ātman* as that which is desirable or worth cherishing *par excellence*, can be traced as far back as the Upaniṣads

Here a basic doubt may be posed as to how far philosophy could and should at all be identified with the quest for value-realization. Perhaps it could be treated as a legitimate, and open, question. But in any case a counter-question might as well be urged whether a value-neutral attitude of pure analysis and distinguishment of essence or meaning would prove to be enough for philosophic consciousness. Perhaps it might be urged : intellectual clarity alone is not self-sufficient and self-explanatory, in the long run—'clarity is not enought' (as H. H. Price perhaps would have put it). If it were not enough, should not the value-interest, in its depth, be integrated to philosophic reflection, rather than being looked upon as something inherently unamenable to it ?

Coming, then, to the so-called subjective attitude itself (in a genuinely philosophical, not psychological, sense), one might still linger with the root question : why at all start with the subjective attitude, instead of the commonly accepted objective attitude ? And if starting with that attitude, why commit to it in philosophizing ? The question has been touched upon in the beginning of our enquiry. Here it may be urged that such an attitude remains, after all, an original starting-point in philosophy. It is worth recalling in this connexion how Kant proposed in his so-called "Copernican Revolution" a turn in the way of thinking (*Denkart*) in his first *Critique*. And Husserl was all the more pronounced in his prescription of a 'bracketing' of what he considers to be the naive belief in objective reality of existent facts (through 'transcendental epoché'). However, both in Kantian transcendentalism as well as in phenomenology the proposed reversion of the natural (objective) attitude in philosophic reflection, though deliberate in a sense, has admittedly been *theoretic* in motive and character.

Coming back to Vedānta, the recommended transformation of the common objective attitude has been basically value-

(see, for example, *Bṛhadāraṇyaka* Up., IV. ii. 5 : "*Ātmanastu kāmāya sarvam priyam bhavati*" etc). But somehow this trend seems to have been in itself far less developed than its doctrine of *Cit-cum-Sat*. Within the range of present discourse too the concept of *Ānanda* has not been taken into consideration, although I am fully aware it opens up a significant dimension in an in-depth critique of experience, and as such is worth a separate investigation.

motivated and deeply oriented in a tradition of philosophical culture, rather than one primarily theoretic in outlook.* Consequently, though the subjectively-oriented metaphysic of experience did not exclusively develop in the direction of a thoroughgoing critique of knowledge—as in Kant or in Phenomenology so conspicuously—Vedānta, nonetheless, has been in a position to yield a philosophy of subjectivity in concrete (beyond the epistemic), which finds its ontological grounding by overstepping itself on the edges of transcendental experience. This concreteness of standpoint, in that sense, might seem to have been gained at the cost of a purely theoretico-methodological interest in the analysis of knowledge and experience. But, then, that is what Advaita Vedānta stands for.

Thus the question of accent on subjectivity—the approach through the subjective beyond subjectivity itself—is geared to a deeper value-interest (not, again, an interest in the theory of values). But the said interest—existential as it characteristically is—is yet not sought to be met, within the system of Vedāntic thought and culture, by way of an 'irrationalistic' commitment of any sort. Rather than expressing a mere 'attitude to life', which could as well be non-cognitive in its principal thrust, Vedanta brings forward an essentially cognitive—or meta-cognitive, as it proves to be in the long run—legitimation of the underlying value-drive. And the latter reflects totally the concern of life-practice at its deepest.

*For an intensive discussion of the issue of theory vis-a-vis prartice as it pertains to classical Indian thought, in contrast to the general character of Western philosophy, in the light of Husserl's reflections on that subject from the phenomenological perspective, reference may be made to my article "Theory and practice in Indian thought : Husserl's observations", published in : *Philosophy East and West*. vol. 21, No. 3.

SELECT BIBLIOGRAPHY (OF SANSKRIT WORKS)*

[The list includes only the texts of Advaita Vedānta which have been referred to in this book. The texts belonging to other Indian systems such as Nyāya-Vaiśeṣika, Sāṅkhya-Yoga, Mīmāṃsā, Buddhism etc. are not separately mentioned here.]

Brahmasūtra Śāṅkara-Bhāṣya, with *Bhāmatī*, *Kalpataru* and *Parimala*. Ed. by A. Sastri, Nirnaya Sagar Pr., Bombay, 1938. (S.B.B.S.). Rept. Motilal Banarsidass, Delhi, 1980.

Śāṅkara-Bhāṣya on *Bṛhadāraṇyaka Upaniṣad* (S.B.Br.Up.).

Śāṅkara-Bhāṣya on *Māṇḍūkya Upaniṣad*, and on *Māṇḍūkya-kārikā* of Gauḍapāda. (S. B. Māṇḍ-Up.; S. B. Māṇḍ. Kar.).

Śāṅkara-Bhāṣya on *Kaṭha Upaniṣad* (S. B. Kaṭha. Up.).

Pañcapādikā of Padmapāda, Vizianagram Sanskrit Series (No. 3) Benares, 1891.

Pañcapādikāvivaraṇa of Prakāśātman, V. S. Series (No. 5), Benares, 1892. (*Vivaraṇa*). Also : *Pañcapādikā*, with *Prabodha-pariśodhinī* of Ātmasvarūpa and *Tātparyārthadyotinī* of Vijñānātman; and *Pañcapādikāvivaraṇa*, with *Tātparyadīpikā* of Citsukhācārya and *Bhāvaprakāśikā* of Nṛsiṃhāśrama—edited by S. Srirama Sastri and S. R. Krishnamurti Sastri, Govt. Oriental Manuscripts Library, Madras, 1958.

Vivaraṇaprameyasaṅgraha of Vidyāraṇya, V. S. S. (No. 7), Benares, 1893.

Pañcadaśī of Vidyāraṇya, with *Rāmakṛṣṇa-ṭīkā*, Nirnaya Sagar, 1905.

Vedāntasāra of Sadānanda, with *Bālabodhinī-ṭīkā*, Ed. by K. S. Aiyar, Srirangam, 1911; Ed. by M. Hiriyanna, Oriental Book Agency, Poona, 1929.

*References to the relevant Indian and Western literature—along with necessary citations—are given in *Notes and References* attached to the respective chapters, as well as in the running foot-notes.

Tattvapradipikā (*Citsukhī*) of Citsukha, with *Nayanaprasādinītikā*, Ed. by K. Shastri, Nirnaya Sagar. (*Citsukhī*).

Tattvaśuddhi by Jñānaghana, Ed. by Shastri and Radhakrishnan University of Madras.

Vedāntasiddhāntamuktāvalī of *Prakāśānanda*, Ed. by A. Venis, Benares, 1922.

Advaitadīpikā of Nṛsiṃhāśrama, pub. Lazarus, Benares.

Vedāntaparibhāṣā of Dharmarāja Adhvarīndra, Ed. by A. Sastri, Calcutta University, 1927.

Siddhāntaleśasaṅgraha of Appaya Dīkṣita, Ed. by S. S. S. Sastri, University of Madras.

Sarvadarśanasaṅgraha of Mādhava, Ed. by V. Shastri, Bhandarkar Oriental Research Institute, Poona, 1924.

INDEX